EXODUS & NUMBERS

The Exodus from Egypt

John MacArthur

THOMAS NELSON
Since 1798

MacArthur Bible Studies

Exodus & Numbers: The Exodus from Egypt

© 2015 by John MacArthur

Originally published as *The Exodus From Egypt: Moses and God's Mercy.*

Published in Nashville, Tennessee, by Nelson Books, an imprint of Thomas Nelson. Nelson Books and Thomas Nelson are registered trademarks of HarperCollins Christian Publishing, Inc.

Originally published in association with the literary agency of Wolgemuth & Associates, Inc. Original layout, design, and writing assistance by Gregory C. Benoit Publishing, Old Mystic, Connecticut.

"Unleashing God's Truth, One Verse at a Time®" is a trademark of Grace to You. All rights reserved.

Thomas Nelson titles may be purchased in bulk for educational, business, fundraising, or sales promotional use. For information, please e-mail SpecialMarkets@ThomasNelson.com.

Scripture quotations are taken from *The New King James Version.* © 1982 by Thomas Nelson. Used by permission. All rights reserved.

Some material from the Introduction, "Keys to the Text" and "Exploring the Meaning" sections taken from *The MacArthur Bible Commentary,* John MacArthur. Copyright © 2005 Thomas Nelson Publishers.

ISBN 978-0-7180-3470-2

First Printing December 2015 / Printed in the United States of America

HB 05.21.2024

CONTENTS

Introduction

1. The Selection of Moses   1
   Exodus 3:1–4:17

2. Confronting Pharaoh   13
   Exodus 5:1–6:9; 9:1–35

3. The First Passover   25
   Exodus 12:1–51

4. Crossing the Red Sea   37
   Exodus 14:1–31

5. The Law of God   49
   Exodus 20:1–21

6. Moses on the Mountain   61
   Exodus 33:1–34:35

7. Building the Tabernacle   73
   Exodus 35:1–36:38; 39:32–40:43

8. Complaints and Rebellion   85
   Numbers 11:1–12:16

9. At the Doorstep   97
   Numbers 13:16–14:38

10. No Water in the Wilderness   109
    Numbers 20:1–29

11. Balaam and Balak   121
    Numbers 22:1–23:30; 25:1–3

12. Reviewing Key Principles   133

INTRODUCTION

At the end of the book of Genesis, Joseph led his family to settle in the rich lands of Goshen in Egypt to escape the great famine that was plaguing all the land (see Genesis 47). The Israelites originally settled there as guests of the king, but over time their growing numbers made the Egyptians concerned that in the event of war they would rise up against them. So they made the Hebrew people their slaves.

The Israelites remained in this state for most of the 430 years they spent in Egypt. However, the Lord had promised Abraham that his descendants would one day be led out of their slavery and back into the land of Canaan. Our studies begin when that time had finally arrived. The Lord began guiding His people out of Egypt by selecting a man to lead them: Moses, one of the most humble men in Scripture.

During their travels toward Canaan, the people of Israel witnessed the power and faithfulness of God in countless ways. He went with them physically in a pillar of cloud by day and a pillar of fire by night. He met with Moses face to face on Mount Sinai. He provided food and water and delivered the people from the most deadly army on earth. Yet despite all these miracles (and many more), the people of Israel constantly grumbled and complained against God and Moses.

In these twelve studies, we will examine the biblical events depicted in the books of Exodus and Numbers. We will examine God's calling of Moses, the ten plagues He sent against Egypt, the Ten Commandments He gave to the people, the miraculous provisions He brought in the wilderness, and much more. We will also learn some precious truths about the character of God and see His great faithfulness in keeping His promises. We will learn, in short, what it means to walk by faith.

THE BOOK OF EXODUS

The book of Exodus was so named in the Septuagint (the Greek translation of the Bible) and the Latin Vulgate of the Old Testament because the departure of Israel from Egypt is the dominant historical fact of the book. In the Hebrew Bible, the opening words, "And (or now) these are the names," served as the title of the book. The opening *and* or *now* in the Hebrew title suggests the book was to be accepted as the obvious sequel to Genesis, the first book of Moses. Hebrews 11:22 commends the faith of Joseph who, while on his deathbed (c. 1804 BC), spoke of the "departure" or the "exiting" of the sons of Israel, looking ahead more than 350 years to the exodus.

AUTHOR

Mosaic authorship of Exodus is affirmed in Scripture. Moses followed God's instructions and "wrote all the words of the LORD" (24:4), which included the record of the battle with Amalek (17:14), the Ten Commandments (34:4, 27–29), and the Book of the Covenant (20:22–23:33). Similar assertions of Mosaic writing occur elsewhere in the Pentateuch, and the Old Testament corroborates Mosaic authorship of the portions mentioned above. The New Testament concurs by (1) citing Exodus 3:6 as part of "the book of Moses" (Mark 12:26), (2) assigning Exodus 13:2 to "the law of Moses," which is also referred to as "the law of the Lord" (Luke 2:22–23), (3) ascribing Exodus 20:12 and 21:17 to Moses (Mark 7:10), (4) attributing the law to Moses (John 7:19; Romans 10:5), and (5) by Jesus' specifically declaring that Moses had written of Him (John 5:46–47).

DATE

Moses wrote Exodus sometime after the Israelites' departure from Egypt but obviously before his death on Mount Nebo. Scripture dates Solomon's fourth year of reign (c. 965 BC) as being 480 years after the exodus (see 1 Kings 6:1), thus establishing the date of 1445 BC for the exodus. The judge Jephthah also noted that by his day, Israel had possessed Heshbon for 300 years (see Judges

11:26). Calculating backward and forward from Jephthah—and taking into account different periods of foreign oppression, judgeships and kingships, the wilderness wanderings, and the initial entry and conquest of Canaan—amounts to 480 years and confirms the date of 1445 BC.

BACKGROUND AND SETTING

Moses, born in 1525 BC, spent the first forty years of his life in the courts of Pharaohs Thutmose I and II and Queen Hatshepsut. He spent the next forty years in self-imposed exile during the reign of Thutmose III, before returning to be Israel's leader early during the reign of Amenhotep II, the pharaoh of the exodus. God used both the educational system of Egypt and Moses' exile in Midian to prepare him to guide the Israelites through the wilderness of the Sinai Peninsula during his final forty years. Moses died on Mount Nebo when he was 120 years old, and though he looked on the Promised Land from afar, he never entered it. Centuries later, he appeared to the disciples on the Mount of Transfiguration (see Matthew 17:3).

HISTORICAL AND THEOLOGICAL THEMES

The exodus marked the beginning of the fulfillment of God's covenant promise to Abraham that his descendants would not only reside in the Promised Land but also multiply and become a great nation (see Genesis 12:1–3, 7). The book traces the rapid growth of Jacob's descendants from Egypt to the establishment of the theocratic nation in their Promised Land. It also recounts how at appropriate times, such as on Mount Sinai and in the plains of Moab, God gave the Israelites a body of legislation (the Law), which they needed in order to live in Israel as His people. By this, they were distinct from other nations. Through God's self-revelation, the Israelites were instructed in the sovereignty and majesty, the goodness and holiness, and the grace and mercy of their Lord, the one and only God of heaven and earth.

INTERPRETIVE CHALLENGES

The absence of any Egyptian record of the devastation of Egypt by the ten plagues and the major defeat of Pharaoh's army at the Red Sea should not give rise to speculation on whether the account is authentic. Egyptian historiography did not permit records of their pharaohs' embarrassments and ignominious defeats to be published. In addition, despite the absence of extra-biblical records of the Hebrew bondage, the plagues, the exodus, and the conquest, the archeological evidence corroborates the early date. All pharaohs of the fifteenth century left evidence of interest in building enterprises in Lower Egypt, and these projects were accessible to Moses in the region near Goshen.

The typological significance of the tabernacle has occasioned much reflection. Ingenuity in linking every item of furniture and every piece of building material to Christ may appear most intriguing; however, if New Testament statements and allusions do not support such linkage and typology, hermeneutical caution must rule. The tabernacle's structure and ornamentation for efficiency and beauty is one thing, but finding hidden meaning and symbolism is unfounded. How the sacrificial and worship system of the tabernacle and its parts typify the redeeming work of the coming Messiah must be left to those New Testament passages that treat the subject.

THE BOOK OF NUMBERS

The English title "Numbers" comes from the Septuagint and Latin Vulgate of the Old Testament. This designation is based on the numberings that constitute a major focus of some of the chapters. The most common Hebrew title comes from the fifth word in the Hebrew text of Numbers 1:1, "in the wilderness [of]." This name is much more descriptive of the total contents of the book, which recount the history of Israel during almost thirty-nine years of wandering in the wilderness. Another Hebrew title, favored by some early church fathers, is based on the first word of the Hebrew text of 1:1: "and He spoke." This designation emphasizes that the book records the word of God to Israel.

AUTHOR

The first five books of the Bible, called the Law, are ascribed to Moses throughout Scripture (see Joshua 8:31; 2 Kings 14:6; Nehemiah 8:1; Mark 12:26; John 7:19). The book of Numbers itself refers to the writing of Moses in 33:2 and 36:13.

DATE

Moses wrote Numbers during the final year of his life, and the events from Numbers 20:1 to the end of the book occur during the fortieth year after the exodus. The account ends with Israel poised on the eastern side of the Jordan River across from Jericho, which is where the conquest of the land of Canaan began. Numbers must be dated c. 1405 BC, as it is foundational to the book of Deuteronomy, which is dated in the eleventh month of the fortieth year after the exodus (see Deuteronomy 1:3).

BACKGROUND AND SETTING

Most of the events of the book are set "in the wilderness," which refers to land that contains little vegetation or trees and, because of a lack of rainfall, cannot be cultivated. This land is best used for tending flocks of animals. In Numbers 1:1–10:10, Israel encamped in the wilderness in Sinai. It was at Sinai the Lord had entered into the Mosaic covenant with them. From 10:11–12:16, Israel traveled from Sinai to Kadesh. In 13:1–20:13, the events took place in and around Kadesh, which was located in the wilderness of Paran and the wilderness of Zin. From 20:14–22:1, Israel traveled from Kadesh to the plains of Moab. All the events of 22:2–36:13 occurred while Israel was encamped in the plain to the north of Moab. That plain was a flat and fertile piece of land in the middle of the wasteland.

The book of Numbers concentrates on events that take place in the second and fortieth years after the exodus. The incidents recorded in Numbers 1:1–14:45 all occur in 1444 BC, the year after the exodus. Everything referred to after 20:1 is dated c. 1406/1405 BC, the fortieth year after the exodus. The laws and events found in 15:1–19:22 is undated, but probably should be dated c. 1443 to 1407 BC. The lack of material devoted to this thirty-seven year period, in comparison with the other years of the journey from Egypt to Canaan, communicates how wasted those years were because of Israel's rebellion against the Lord and His consequent judgment.

HISTORICAL AND THEOLOGICAL THEMES

Numbers chronicles the experiences of two generations of the nation of Israel. The first generation participated in the exodus from Egypt. They were numbered for the war of conquest, but when they arrived at the southern edge of Canaan, they refused to enter. Because of their rebellion against the Lord, all the adults aged twenty and older (except Caleb and Joshua) were sentenced to die in the wilderness. In Numbers 15–25, this generation dies out and the second grows to adulthood. A second numbering of the people takes place, and these Israelites do go to war and inherit the Promised Land.

Three theological themes permeate Numbers. First, the Lord Himself communicated to Israel through Moses, so the words of Moses had divine authority. Israel's response to Moses mirrored her obedience to the Lord. Numbers contains three distinct divisions based on Israel's response to the word of the Lord: (1) obedience (chapters 1–10), (2) disobedience (chapters 11–25), and (3) renewed obedience (chapters 26–36). The second theme is that the Lord is the God of judgment. Throughout Numbers, the anger of the Lord is aroused in response to Israel's sin. A third theme is the faithfulness of the Lord to keep His promise to give the seed of Abraham the land of Canaan.

INTERPRETIVE CHALLENGES

Four interpretive challenges face the reader of Numbers. The first is whether Numbers is to be considered a separate book or part of a larger literary whole of the Pentateuch. The biblical books of Genesis, Exodus, Leviticus, Numbers, and Deuteronomy form the Torah, and the remainder of the Scripture always views these five books as a unit. The ultimate meaning of Numbers thus cannot be divorced from its context in the Pentateuch. However, every Hebrew manuscript divides the Pentateuch the same way as the present text, with Numbers being a well-defined unit with a structural integrity of its own. The book has its own beginning, middle, and ending, even as it functions within a larger whole. Thus, Numbers is also to be viewed with singular identity.

The second challenge is whether there is a sense of coherence in the book of Numbers. It is readily evident that Numbers contains a wide variety of literary materials and forms, including census lists, genealogies, laws, historical narratives, poetry, prophecy, and travel lists. Nevertheless, they are all blended into a cohesive whole to tell the story of Israel's journey from Mount Sinai to the plains of Moab.

A third challenge deals with the large numbers of people given for the tribes of Israel in Numbers 1:46 and 26:51. These two lists of Israel's men of war, taken thirty-nine years apart, both put the number at more than 600,000. These numbers demand a total population for Israel in the wilderness of around 2.5 million at any one time. From a natural perspective, this seems too high for the wilderness conditions to sustain. However, it must be recognized that the Lord supernaturally took care of Israel for forty years. Therefore, the large numbers must be accepted at face value.

The fourth interpretive challenge concerns the heathen prophet Balaam, whose story is recorded in Numbers 22:2–24:25. Even though Balaam claimed to know the Lord, the Bible consistently refers to him as a false prophet. The Lord used Balaam as His mouthpiece to speak the true words He put in his mouth.

THE EXODUS FROM EGYPT

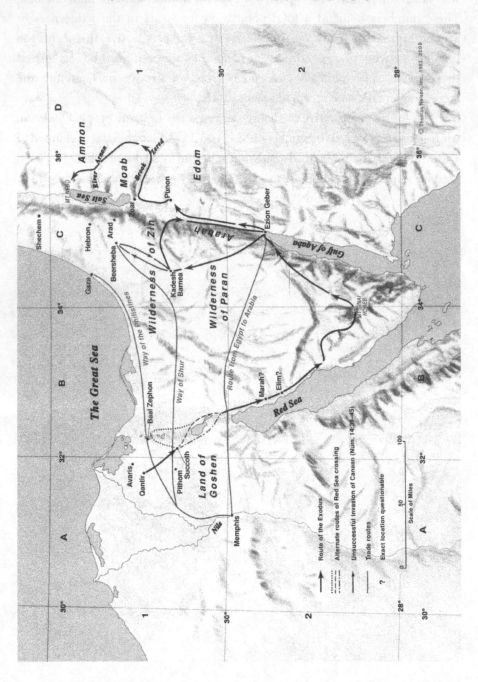

Route of the Exodus

Alternate routes of Red Sea crossing

Unsuccessful invasion of Canaan (Num. 14:39–45)

Trade routes

Exact location questionable

Scale of Miles
0   50   100

© Thomas Nelson, Inc. 1983, 2008

THE SELECTION OF MOSES

Exodus 3:1–4:17

DRAWING NEAR

From a human perspective, Moses was an unlikely choice to lead the people of Israel. What characteristics does our society tend to look for in a leader?

_____

_____

_____

THE CONTEXT

The Israelites (also known as the Hebrews) had been living in Egypt for more than four hundred years, and they had been slaves for much of that time. But even during their slavery the Lord had blessed His people, and their numbers had grown dramatically. In fact, they became so numerous that Pharaoh, the ruler of Egypt, began to fear they would become a threat to his nation. So he devised a murderous plan: all males born to the Hebrews would be put to death immediately.

This evil king set his plan in motion to put an end to the Hebrew race. But the Lord had other ideas. First, He caused the Egyptian midwives to lie to the king. They told him that the Hebrew women were so strong they gave birth *without* the midwives' aid. Then God used Pharaoh's wicked act to move one significant Hebrew baby—Moses—into the house of Pharaoh himself.

Moses was brought up in the royal Egyptian court. This provided him with a top-notch education, exposure to the highest levels of government, and connections within the king's court. It also removed him from the hardships of his people—for a time. But the Lord did not permit him to become complacent in his role, and He never let Moses forget that he, too, was a Hebrew.

One day, Moses saw an Egyptian slave driver abusing a Hebrew. He intervened, killed the Egyptian, and buried him in the sand—but his deed did not go unnoticed. So, fearing for his life, Moses fled into the wilderness to start a new life in Midian. There he married and settled down to live comfortably as a shepherd.

But again, the Lord had other plans. He had ordained all the circumstances of Moses' life to prepare him for one momentous task: leading the Israelites out of bondage and into the Promised Land. This would be an intimidating and costly calling for Moses, but the Lord would be with him each step of the way.

KEYS TO THE TEXT

Read Exodus 3:1–4:17, noting the key words and phrases indicated below.

THE BURNING BUSH: While Moses' fellow Hebrews have been toiling under cruel Egyptian taskmasters, he has spent forty years working as a shepherd. All of that was about to change.

3:1. MOSES: Moses was born a Hebrew but had been raised in the household of Pharaoh, where he received the best education and upbringing of his day. "Now it came to pass in those days, when Moses was grown, that he went out to his brethren and looked at their burdens. And he saw an Egyptian beating a Hebrew, one of his brethren. So . . . he killed the Egyptian and hid him in the sand" (Exodus 2:11–12). Moses then fled Egypt, met a priest in Midian, and married his daughter Zipporah. He lived comfortably in Midian for forty years. This is where our study begins.

HOREB, THE MOUNTAIN OF GOD: Mount Sinai, located in the mountainous region between the Red Sea and the Gulf of Aqaba (see the map in the Introduction).

2. THE ANGEL OF THE LORD: This phrase appears frequently throughout the book of Exodus. It describes what is called a *theophany*, or a "pre-incarnate appearance" of God prior to the birth of Christ.

THE BUSH WAS BURNING WITH FIRE, BUT THE BUSH WAS NOT CONSUMED: Moses' attention was drawn to a most unusual sight: a burning bush that was not being burnt up by the fire within its branches. Even more amazing for Moses was the fact that God would address him through this bush.

3. I WILL NOW TURN ASIDE AND SEE THIS GREAT SIGHT: Scholars have attempted to find some natural explanation for the burning bush, such as certain types of flowers with gaseous pods. But Moses had been working in that desert region for forty years and would have been familiar with the regional flora. He certainly would not have commented on something mundane. This incident was so unusual that he stopped what he was doing to investigate further. A supernatural event is the only viable explanation.

GOD SPEAKS TO MOSES: *The Lord Himself is present in the burning bush, and He speaks directly to Moses to outline His plans.*

5. DO NOT DRAW NEAR THIS PLACE: God's presence is utterly holy, and He will not permit sinful man to draw near Him. We will see this throughout the Israelites' interactions with God: those who approached Him casually risked being struck dead. Christians today have the privilege of entering boldly into God's presence, but this is only because we do so through the redeeming blood of Christ.

6. THE GOD OF ABRAHAM, THE GOD OF ISAAC, AND THE GOD OF JACOB: The Lord promised Abraham that He would make a great nation of him, with descendants that outnumbered the stars in the sky (see Genesis 15:5). But He also said, "Your descendants will be strangers in a land that is not theirs, and will serve them, and they will afflict them four hundred years. And also the nation whom they serve I will judge; afterward they shall come out with great possessions" (verses 13–14). Moses did not know it yet, but he was about to participate in the fulfillment of that promise by leading the descendants of Abraham out of Egypt.

MOSES HID HIS FACE, FOR HE WAS AFRAID TO LOOK UPON GOD: We will see this theme reiterated throughout our studies. Moses would later ask to see God's glory, but the Lord would warn him that no one could see His face and live. Moses would also spend time in the Lord's presence in days to come. His own face would glow so brightly that he would have to wear a veil.

7. I KNOW THEIR SORROWS: The Israelites' circumstances were not a surprise to God. He knew what their situation would be long before it happened, and it was all part of a plan that He had established "before the foundation of the world" (Ephesians 1:4). Nevertheless, He was still paying close attention to His people's circumstances, and His heart was moved by their plight. He had sent them to Egypt for a purpose, sustained them in their bondage, and would be faithful to carry them back to Canaan.

8. TO A GOOD AND LARGE LAND: God's descriptions of the Promised Land emphatically underscored the land-promise of the Abrahamic covenant.

FLOWING WITH MILK AND HONEY: A formal and graphic way of describing a fertile land of bounteous provision.

THE CANAANITES AND THE HITTITES: A specific identification of the territory to which Israel was going. Other people currently inhabited her Promised Land.

MOSES' FIRST EXCUSE: Moses understandably feels inadequate for the great assignment God is giving to him. But the Lord promises to overcome his weaknesses.

11. WHO AM I THAT I SHOULD GO: On the one hand, Moses was making a realistic assessment of himself. He had been away from Egypt for forty years, was living in the desert regions as a shepherd, and was a member of a class of people despised by the Egyptians (see Genesis 46:33–34). On the other hand, the Lord had specifically ordained events in Moses' life to prepare him for this leadership role, including his growing up in Pharaoh's household. This gave Moses access to the king's court, as he was remembered there. No other Hebrew had that access.

12. I WILL CERTAINLY BE WITH YOU: God made this same promise to Abraham, Isaac, and Jacob, and He fulfilled it beyond their expectations. He had consistently proven Himself faithful to His Word and to His people. This promise alone should have been sufficient to give Moses confidence.

13. WHAT IS HIS NAME: Here Moses raised another objection: the Hebrews might ask for God's name to validate that he had been sent by the God of

their fathers. Significantly, the question was not, "Who is this God?" The Hebrews knew the name *Yahweh* (as Genesis well indicates). Asking "who" would be inquiring about title, name, and identity, whereas "what" inquired into the character, quality, or essence of a person. God answered Moses' question by pointing to His divine, eternal character.

14. I AM WHO I AM: The almighty God, who created all that exists, is beyond the comprehension of mankind. He always was, always is, always shall be, and is unchanging and unfathomable. He is who He is.

16. ELDERS: Literally "bearded ones," which indicated the age and wisdom needed to lead.

SAY TO THEM: The Lord laid out for Moses all that would happen before Pharaoh released the Israelites and provided him with two speeches: one for Israel's elders and one for Pharaoh himself. Also included was notification of the elders' positive response to Moses' report, of Pharaoh's refusal to grant them their request, and of God's miraculous and judgmental reaction.

18. THREE DAYS' JOURNEY: This request to allow the Hebrews a three-day journey into the wilderness to worship God was not a ruse to get the people out and not return. Rather, it was an initial moderate request to highlight the intransigence of Pharaoh. He would not let his slaves leave under any conditions!

22. YOU SHALL PLUNDER THE EGYPTIANS: God told Moses the people would leave Egypt carrying great wealth from their former slave masters. This may have seemed far-fetched to Moses at the time, but it was in keeping with the promise God had given to Abraham hundreds of years earlier: "The nation whom they serve I will judge; afterward they shall come out with great possessions" (Genesis 15:14).

A SERIES OF MIRACULOUS SIGNS: The Lord gives Moses several dramatic signs with which to prove that he is speaking the words of God.

4:1. BUT SUPPOSE: The Lord had revealed many things to Moses at this point. He had told Moses His name, despite the boldness of the request. He had divulged many details of the future, including the fact the Israelites would eventually leave Egypt with great wealth. Most significantly, the Lord had promised Moses that He would be with him and give him the ability to accomplish the great task of leading His people out of bondage. He had patiently answered each of Moses' questions, offering him reassurances in the face of his hesitancy—but here Moses crossed the line into unbelief.

THE LORD HAS NOT APPEARED TO YOU: God had already told Moses the people would *not* respond this way: the elders would heed his voice (see Genesis 3:18). From a human perspective, however, it is easy to understand Moses' concerns. There is no record that the Lord had appeared to the Israelites during their entire time in Egypt—a period of more than four centuries.

2. WHAT IS THAT IN YOUR HAND: In response to Moses' hypothetical situation of Israel not believing God had appeared to him, the Lord gave Moses three signs to accredit him as the chosen spokesman and leader. Two of these signs would personally involve Moses right then and there.

3. IT BECAME A SERPENT: The devil had used a literal serpent in the garden of Eden to deceive Eve into eating the forbidden fruit. Here, the Lord demonstrated His power over the devil and his evil forces by having Moses cast the serpent to the ground and then pick it up by the tail without being bitten. The miracle showed Moses that God could use anything—even the very wickedness of Satan—to further His own purposes.

5. THAT THEY MAY BELIEVE: Note the purpose God stated for doing these signs: "That they may believe that the LORD God . . . appeared to you."

6. HIS HAND WAS LEPROUS: Leprosy can give us a picture of sin, as the smallest spot of the disease spreads throughout the body and infects everything it touches. This miracle prefigured some of the plagues that would be sent upon Egypt.

9. IF THEY DO NOT BELIEVE EVEN THESE TWO SIGNS: No matter what situation Moses could envision himself facing, God revealed that He had sufficient resources to authenticate His man. Moses was not to think otherwise.

MORE EXCUSES: *The Lord has provided dramatic signs and promises to encourage Moses in his work, but Moses is still not satisfied. He continues to make excuses.*

10. I AM NOT ELOQUENT . . . BUT AM SLOW OF SPEECH: This is a bold statement for Moses to make to God. Indeed it is almost accusatory, as

it suggests that in all of God's miracles, He had failed to heal Moses' speech defects. Adam used a similar ploy when God confronted him with his sin, suggesting that somehow his failure was God's fault: "The woman *whom You gave to be with me*, she gave me of the tree, and I ate" (Genesis 3:12, emphasis added). Moses was trying to find excuses for not obeying God, and his final attempt was to blame God Himself.

11. WHO HAS MADE MAN'S MOUTH: The Lord sometimes used rhetorical questions when confronting mankind's impudence (see Job 38).

12. I WILL BE WITH YOUR MOUTH: The Lord had been immensely patient with Moses' excuses, promising again and again that He would work through even Moses' weaknesses and shortcomings. "But when they deliver you up, do not worry about how or what you should speak. For it will be given to you in that hour what you should speak; for it is not you who speak, but the Spirit of your Father who speaks in you" (Matthew 10:19–20).

13. BUT HE SAID: Moses' previous concerns were merely excuses to cover the fact that he simply did not want to do what the Lord was commanding him to do. Here he was finally making his intentions clear, and his final answer was, "Send someone else!"

14. THE ANGER OF THE LORD WAS KINDLED AGAINST MOSES: God had repeatedly extended grace and encouragement to Moses. But He will not withhold His anger indefinitely when His people persist in refusing to obey His word.

AARON . . . YOUR BROTHER: The Lord agreed to send both Moses and Aaron to lead His people out of slavery, but this was a concession to Moses' stubbornness rather than His original intention. Aaron would prove to be both an asset and a liability to Moses' leadership.

15. I WILL TEACH YOU: The use here of the plural pronoun *you* means that God had promised to assist both Aaron and Moses in their newly appointed duties.

16. YOU SHALL BE TO HIM AS GOD: That is, the Lord would speak to Moses directly, and Moses would tell Aaron what to say. This was the pattern throughout the wilderness wanderings after the people left Egypt.

17. THIS ROD . . . WITH WHICH YOU SHALL DO THE SIGNS: Moses, despite God's anger at his unwillingness, retained superiority in that he had the instrument by which miracles would be done.

Unleashing the Text

1) If you had been in Moses' position, how would you have responded to God's command to lead the Israelites out of Egypt?

_____

_____

_____

2) What were Moses' fears and concerns? How did the Lord answer those issues?

_____

_____

_____

3) How had the Lord prepared Moses for this big assignment? How did He sovereignly use circumstances and "chance events" (humanly speaking) for that purpose?

_____

_____

_____

4) Read Hebrews 11:23–29. What was Moses giving up by obeying God's command? What did his obedience cost him? What did he gain?

_____

_____

_____

EXPLORING THE MEANING

God will graciously empower us for whatever work He calls us to do. Moses apparently suffered from some sort of speech defect. He may have stuttered, as traditional Jewish writers have suggested, or he may simply have felt that he was not eloquent. Whatever the cause, he was convinced that he could not fulfill the great assignment God was calling him to perform.

Yet the Lord promised Moses, at each objection, that He would strengthen his weakness and overcome his shortcomings. "Have I not made your mouth?" the Lord asked. "Do I not know your strengths and weaknesses? It is *My* power, not yours, which shall set My people free."

The Lord may sometimes call us to do tasks that seem beyond our ability. What we must remember is that it is not *we* who are at work but the power of His Holy Spirit within us. He can use even our weaknesses to bring about His glory, and He will never call us to do something that we cannot do with His help.

The Lord wants our obedience, not our excuses. This does not mean we should not pour out our concerns before the Lord. Moses certainly had some legitimate questions, such as what he should say and how he would establish his credentials. The Lord patiently addressed those concerns and repeatedly promised that He would work out the details—that He would, in fact, be right beside Moses each step of the way.

But Moses' real concern had less to do with his inadequacy than with his desires: he simply didn't *want* to obey. He certainly had reasons for not wanting to return to Egypt. He had killed a man there and might still face arrest. He had established a comfortable life in Midian, working for his father-in-law as a shepherd. There is no question the Lord was calling him to uproot himself and get out of his "comfort zone."

However, when the Lord calls us, our job is to obey—even if it seems inconvenient or unfamiliar. When the Lord calls us to do something difficult, we must be honest in prayer and pour out our fears and concerns before His throne of grace. But once we have expressed our concerns, the final step is to obey. God will provide the power to accomplish what He asks.

The Lord accomplishes great things through weak people. This is the corollary to the previous principle: once we obey, the Lord will use us to accomplish great things for His eternal kingdom. Moses was learning the lesson that it is God's power, not man's, that accomplishes His miraculous plans. What is required of His people is an obedient spirit, not a roster of tremendous gifts and abilities.

The Lord worked several miracles for Moses, turning his shepherd's crook into a serpent and causing his hand to become leprous and then immediately healing it again. But those miracles were nothing compared to the mighty signs and wonders the Lord would show in Egypt and in the wilderness through Moses. But first he had to obey and answer God's call.

The truth is that God often uses "weak" people to accomplish great things. He uses people who are underequipped, from a human perspective, for the specific purpose of showing forth *His* power in their lives. "God has chosen the foolish things of the world to put to shame the wise, and . . . the weak things of the world to put to shame the things which are mighty; and the base things of the world and the things which are despised God has chosen, and the things which are not, to bring to nothing the things that are, that no flesh should glory in His presence" (1 Corinthians 1:27–29).

REFLECTING ON THE TEXT

5) At what point did Moses' questions go from legitimate concerns to stubbornness? How can we distinguish between these two responses in our own hearts?

_____

_____

_____

6) Why did God use the three miracles (the snake, leprosy, and turning water into blood) to encourage Moses? What did they reveal about God's character?

_____

_____

_____

7) How was Moses' mission affected by the fact Aaron would be his spokesman? Did Moses' stubbornness interfere with God's sovereign plans?

_____

_____

_____

8) When has God called you to do something that was outside your comfort zone? How did you respond to that calling?

_____

_____

_____

PERSONAL RESPONSE

9) Is the Lord presently calling you to some difficult act of obedience? Are you making excuses or moving forward?

_____

_____

_____

10) When have you seen the Lord work through or around your own weaknesses? How has He been glorified by your obedience?

_____

_____

_____

_____

2

CONFRONTING PHARAOH

Exodus 5:1–6:9; 9:1–35

DRAWING NEAR

What does the term *hard-hearted* mean today? Why is it generally difficult to deal with a person who is hard-hearted?

_____

_____

_____

THE CONTEXT

Moses returned to Egypt, as the Lord had commanded him. His brother, Aaron, met him along the way—just as God had predicted at the burning bush. The two of them went immediately to the elders of Israel, told them what the Lord had commanded, and showed them the signs the Lord had given Moses. The people then believed and rejoiced, just as the Lord had foretold.

But the battle was not over—in fact, it had not even begun. Moses and Aaron still had to face Pharaoh and demand he release his slaves, and that would not be an easy task. The pharaohs (note *pharaoh* is a title, not a proper name) were the most powerful men in the world and ruled with absolute authority. The Egyptians believed they were descended from the gods and spoke with divine authority on earth. The Hebrews, on the other hand, were mere slaves and people of utterly no account in Egypt. Yet God had called a lowly Hebrew to approach the greatest man on earth—one who thought he was a god—and tell him the true God of his slaves commanded him to set them free!

The Lord had told Moses in advance that Pharaoh would not be open to this idea and that he would deliberately "harden his heart" against God's words. But He had also informed Moses that He would use Pharaoh's stubbornness to show forth His glory to the world, and that in the end He would redeem His people out of bondage. Despite this promise, it still proved a test of faith for Israel and for Moses when the time actually arrived.

KEYS TO THE TEXT

Read Exodus 5:1–6:9, noting the key words and phrases indicated below.

LET MY PEOPLE GO: Moses and Aaron have told the Israelites what the Lord had said to Moses. Now it is time to tell Pharaoh.

1. AFTERWARD: Moses and Aaron went to the elders of the Israelites, told them the words of the Lord, and performed the signs that the Lord had given Moses. "So the people believed; and when they heard that the LORD had visited the children of Israel and that He had looked on their affliction, then they bowed their heads and worshiped" (Exodus 4:31).

2. WHO IS THE LORD: The kings of Egypt believed they were descended from the pagan god Ra, so Pharaoh thought it beneath his dignity to humble himself before the God of the Israelite slaves. His sad inquiry, "Why should I obey His voice?" would soon be resoundingly answered as the Lord sent devastating plagues on Egypt. Yet even then Pharaoh would refuse to humble himself before the almighty God.

4. WHY DO YOU TAKE THE PEOPLE FROM THEIR WORK: Pharaoh obstinately held to his view that the Hebrews were slackers, using Moses' religious request as a ruse to avoid their slave labors. Even in the midst of horrific plagues that demonstrated the reality of God's presence among His people, Pharaoh stubbornly refused to believe the truth of their claims.

THE LAST STRAW: Pharaoh reacts with anger, openly rejecting the lordship of Jehovah. Instead, he increases the slaves' workload.

7. STRAW TO MAKE BRICK: Straw was an essential ingredient in Egyptian brick making, as it was the bonding agent that held the clay together.

8. YOU SHALL LAY ON THEM THE QUOTA OF BRICKS WHICH THEY MADE BEFORE: This was a cruel and harsh response. The people would now have an extra task they did not have previously—the time-and-energy-consuming task of gathering straw. It effectively doubled their efforts, yet they were still responsible for the same number of bricks at the end of the day!

9. LET THEM NOT REGARD FALSE WORDS: Pharaoh presents an excellent picture of the world's system, which continually rejects the Word of God. He was telling the Israelites they were fools for believing in the Lord's words through His servant Moses. They were much better off, he claimed, to accept the religious system around them and not chase after fables. Again, Pharaoh would obstinately insist on this false claim even in the midst of the most incontrovertible proof of God's presence with Israel.

14. THE OFFICERS OF THE CHILDREN OF ISRAEL . . . WERE BEATEN: The Jewish officers probably had grown accustomed to slightly better conditions and treatment than their fellow Hebrews, but they did not escape Pharaoh's wrath. When the world sets itself to oppose the Word of God, all of God's people come under attack.

WE WERE BETTER OFF BEFORE: The people of Israel respond to their suffering by blaming Moses for meddling in their affairs. This will become an unfortunate pattern.

21. YOU HAVE MADE US ABHORRENT IN THE SIGHT OF PHARAOH: The Hebrew leaders were quick to blame Moses and Aaron for their present suffering—even though they had recently endorsed their authority from the Lord.

22. WHY HAVE YOU BROUGHT TROUBLE ON THIS PEOPLE: The Lord had warned Moses that Pharaoh would harden his heart and refuse to let the people leave (see Exodus 3:19–22). The Lord frequently permits His people to experience times of suffering while His plan is unfolding, but He is still entirely in control of all events.

23. NEITHER HAVE YOU DELIVERED YOUR PEOPLE AT ALL: Moses spoke as though he had expected Pharaoh to release the Israelites overnight, but the Lord had warned him that some struggle would be involved. In fact, at this point the struggle had barely even begun. However, once the Lord's glory was revealed, the tussle itself would seem insignificant and brief. Centuries later, the apostle Paul would agree: "For I consider that the sufferings of this present time are not worthy to be compared with the glory which shall be revealed in us" (Romans 8:18).

I AM THE LORD: *The Lord calls the Israelites to change their focus from their sufferings to His character. He is always faithful, even in times of suffering.*

6:1. NOW YOU SHALL SEE WHAT I WILL DO TO PHARAOH: The Lord announced, in response to Moses' prayer, that the stage had been set for dealing with Pharaoh. God had told Moses at the burning bush that His strength would be revealed through Moses' weaknesses. The same would be true of the sufferings of the Israelites: when they were most sorely oppressed, the Lord would reveal His strength on their behalf.

HE WILL DRIVE THEM OUT OF HIS LAND: By the time the plagues finished ravaging Egypt, Pharaoh would not merely consent to the Israelites' leaving but also drive them out. They would leave laden with all the riches of their former slave masters.

2. I AM THE LORD: When the Israelites were most discouraged and their hearts were failing, the Lord reminded them of His character. He is the Lord, Creator of heaven and earth, all-powerful, and yet merciful and loving toward His people. In times of sorrow, the best source of strength and encouragement is to be reminded of God's true nature.

3. BY MY NAME LORD I WAS NOT KNOWN TO THEM: The patriarchs did know the name *Yahweh*, but they had not known the fullness of His character. Each of them—Abraham, Isaac, Jacob, and their forebears—had been admitted into some element of communion and intimacy with God, but Moses and his people would be given a new glimpse of the character of God as He wrought great miracles on their behalf. God was going to reveal Himself more fully and personally to the people of Israel than before.

4. I HAVE ALSO ESTABLISHED MY COVENANT WITH THEM: The Lord had repeatedly promised Abraham and his descendants that they would one day inherit the land of Canaan (for example, see Genesis 15).

5. I HAVE ALSO HEARD THE GROANING OF THE CHILDREN OF ISRAEL: The Israelites were accusing God of oppressing them through Pharaoh's "no-straw" decree, but the truth was just the opposite. He had heard their cries and felt their suffering, and He would not fail to deliver them in keeping with His promises.

7. THEN YOU SHALL KNOW: The Lord does not want us to be content with mere head knowledge concerning His character—He wants us to experience His regenerating power and grace firsthand. The same was true for the Israelites, who were about to experience God's saving power in their physical deliverance from Egypt.

9. THEY DID NOT HEED MOSES: The people of Israel refused to place their faith in God's promises because they were entirely focused on their present sufferings. Today, during such times, it is imperative for us to place our faith in God's Word, remembering that our present trials are temporary but God's glory is eternal.

Read Exodus 9:1–35, noting the key words and phrases indicated below.

THE PLAGUES: When Pharaoh refuses to let the people go, God begins to send plagues on Egypt. Each plague provides Pharaoh with another chance to repent.

1. THEN THE LORD SAID TO MOSES: The Lord had sent four plagues against Egypt: (1) the plague of waters turned to blood (see Exodus 7:20), (2) the plague of frogs (see 8:6), (3) the plague of lice (see 8:17), and the plague of flies (see 8:24). Many of these plagues were associated with various Egyptian deities. For example, the frog was honored as the special representative of an Egyptian goddess, flies were associated with several of their gods, and the sun, which would be completely eclipsed during the ninth plague, was associated with their greatest god, Ra.

2. IF YOU REFUSE TO LET THEM GO, AND STILL HOLD THEM: After each plague, Pharaoh had hardened his heart and refused to heed the word of the Lord.

4. THE LORD WILL MAKE A DIFFERENCE: God demonstrated His faithfulness to His people by sending devastation on the nation of Egypt while protecting His own people in Goshen from suffering at all. It is worth noting that God did this only with certain plagues, while with others He permitted His people to suffer along with the Egyptians. There are times when the Lord allows His people to suffer, but He will never permit us to suffer *true* devastation—Christians will never undergo the wrath of God.

5. THE LORD APPOINTED A SET TIME: The Scriptures tell us that God has appointed set times for all things. He is absolutely in control of all that happens in creation, and when His set time arrives, nothing can prevent His plan from moving forward.

6. ALL THE LIVESTOCK OF EGYPT DIED: That is, all that were in the field, as opposed to any that were contained inside some structure. The Egyptians venerated cattle, especially bulls, and one of their goddesses was represented as part cow.

7. THEN PHARAOH SENT: Pharaoh had been told previous plagues had miraculously spared the Israelites, but this time he investigated himself to see if the reports were true. His findings—proving that the Word of the Lord was indeed truth—should have led him to humble himself and submit to God, but he merely hardened his heart still further. When a man hardens himself against the Word of God, he willfully turns truth into falsehood, and vice versa (see Isaiah 5:20).

10. ASHES FROM THE FURNACE: Moses and Aaron used dust from a lime kiln, the type of furnace the Israelite slaves used to make bricks. Here the Lord took the Egyptians' tool of oppression and used it to damage their own health.

11. THE MAGICIANS: Magic and sorcery played a major role in the pantheistic religious system of Egypt. These magicians were also called "wise men," as they were the learned scientists of their day. They were evidently capable of mimicking some of God's miracles (see, for example, Exodus 7:11), but any power they may have possessed came from Satan rather than God.

COULD NOT STAND BEFORE MOSES: This is a pun. It was literally true in that the men suffered from boils that prevented them from standing comfortably, and it was figuratively true in that they could not mimic this particular miracle, and thus they were disgraced.

GOD HARDENS PHARAOH'S HEART: Thus far, Pharaoh has steadfastly refused to humble himself before God. That pattern eventually becomes unchangeable.

12. THE LORD HARDENED THE HEART OF PHARAOH: This is the first time this wording appears. Pharaoh had persistently refused to humble himself and acknowledge the power of God, so eventually the Lord gave him up to his stubbornness.

13. LET MY PEOPLE GO: Yet even in the midst of Pharaoh's hardened heart, the Lord continued to give him opportunities to repent. We live in the day of God's grace toward mankind, and He is always at work offering people His free gift of salvation. But each time a person refuses, it becomes more difficult to repent.

15. YOU WOULD HAVE BEEN CUT OFF FROM THE EARTH: Even in the midst of sending His judgment against Egypt, the Lord was also showing mercy. Had He poured forth the full fury of His wrath, no man or beast would have survived.

16. FOR THIS PURPOSE I HAVE RAISED YOU UP: Pharaoh believed his authority came from his pagan gods because he was one of their descendants, but Moses boldly stood before him and declared that his authority was granted to him only by the Lord. Further, that authority had been given to him not for his own glory but in order to bring glory to God—to the very God whom Pharaoh was rejecting and resisting.

19. SEND NOW AND GATHER YOUR LIVESTOCK: Once again we see the mercy and grace of God even in the midst of judgment. He forewarned Pharaoh of what plague was coming next and when it would arrive. He told Pharaoh explicitly what he could do to avoid its devastation, just as He had repeatedly told him that the plagues would stop if he would let the Hebrews leave Egypt.

SOME LISTEN, SOME DON'T: Pharaoh and his followers finally confess they have sinned—but only some of them really mean it.

20–21. HE WHO FEARED THE WORD OF THE LORD . . . HE WHO DID NOT: After all the devastation the Lord had rained down on Egypt, it seems hard to believe that people would fail to take so simple a precaution to avoid further loss. Yet this is the nature of man's hardened heart. When a person turns away from God's grace, even common sense cannot soften his heart.

26. IN THE LAND OF GOSHEN: Once again, the Lord sent devastation on the nation of Egypt while miraculously preventing any damage at all on His people.

27. I HAVE SINNED THIS TIME: There is a poignant pathos in this comment, as Pharaoh acknowledged that he had sinned—*this time*. He did not acknowledge that he had sinned previously by stubbornly refusing to release the Israelites, so the Lord knew that he was not truly repentant this time either. As soon as the suffering stopped, he would harden his heart again.

34. HE SINNED YET MORE: Sure enough, after the plague Pharaoh again became resistant and returned to his former sins. This is not true repentance; it is merely an attempt to avoid suffering. True repentance is demonstrated by "turning away" (the literal meaning of the word) from things that displease the Lord.

UNLEASHING THE TEXT

1) Why did the Israelites initially blame Moses for their suffering? If you had been in their place, how would you have responded?

_____

_____

_____

2) Why did Pharaoh persistently refuse to release the Israelites?

_____

_____

_____

3) In what ways did God show His mercy and grace in the midst of His judgments? What does this reveal about His character?

_____

_____

_____

4) Why did God select these specific plagues? What do they reveal about His character? About the Egyptians and their gods?

_____

_____

_____

Exploring the Meaning

Do not harden your heart against God's Word. Pharaoh repeatedly refused to obey God's commands to let the Israelites leave Egypt, yet the Lord continued to give him opportunities to repent. Eventually, however, the Lord gave him over to his hardness of heart, allowing him to remain in stubborn rebellion.

The same principle is true today for the lost world around us. We are living in the day of grace, when salvation is freely available to all who believe, but that day will not last forever. The day is coming when the time for repentance will be past, and all who have rejected Christ will be cast out of the presence of God for all eternity.

It is a dangerous matter to resist God's grace. Each time a person refuses to repent, that repentance becomes more difficult. "For He says: 'In an acceptable time I have heard you, and in the day of salvation I have helped you.' Behold, now is the accepted time; behold, now is the day of salvation" (2 Corinthians 6:2).

God uses discipline and suffering to soften our hearts. The Lord was not being arbitrary when He sent the plagues on Egypt. Each plague was designed to show the Egyptians that there was only one true God and that He was sovereign in the affairs of mankind. God was not pouring out His full wrath on them; in fact, in each plague He demonstrated mercy and grace. His purpose was not to vent His anger but to bring the Egyptians to repentance while simultaneously delivering Israel from their servitude.

The same is true today. The Lord uses hardship to further His purposes in our lives, not to arbitrarily watch us suffer. He uses difficulties to lead people to repentance and salvation, and in the lives of His children to make us more like His Son, Jesus Christ. "My brethren, count it all joy when you fall into various trials, knowing that the testing of your faith produces patience. But let patience have its perfect work, that you may be perfect and complete, lacking nothing" (James 1:2–4).

When the world rebels against God's Word, all His people may suffer. Most of the people of Israel considered themselves innocent bystanders in the struggle between Moses and Pharaoh, and they resented it deeply when they found themselves bearing the brunt of Pharaoh's wrath. They did not recognize they were intimately involved in the struggle because it was actually a struggle between Pharaoh and God.

Pharaoh had set himself up in God's place, and he was determined to prove God had no authority in his life. It was only to be expected, therefore, that he would vent his resentment against the people of God—and all God's people would suffer as a result.

This is often the case, as the New Testament reveals: "If you were of the world, the world would love its own. Yet because you are not of the world, but I chose you out of the world, therefore the world hates you" (John 15:19). "Do not marvel, my brethren, if the world hates you" (1 John 3:13). The Israelites' suffering was for a short duration and was nothing compared to the glory that was revealed when they were released from bondage.

REFLECTING ON THE TEXT

5) What does it mean that "the Lord hardened the heart of Pharaoh"
(Exodus 9:12)? If God hardened Pharaoh's heart, in what way was
Pharaoh still responsible for his own actions?

_____

_____

_____

6) Why did the Lord permit Pharaoh to persecute His people in the first
place? What effect did the persecution have on them?

_____

_____

_____

7) Pharaoh confessed that he had sinned, yet the Lord sent further
plagues. Why? What does it indicate about the sincerity (or lack
thereof) of Pharaoh's sorrow?

_____

_____

_____

8) What does it mean to "harden your heart" against God? Give some
practical examples. Why is this a dangerous practice?

_____

_____

_____

PERSONAL RESPONSE

9) Have you ever hardened your heart toward God? Have you repented of your sins or merely tried to avoid suffering?

_____

_____

_____

10) When have you seen the Lord using difficult or painful circumstances in your life to bring good? How have you responded during such times of hardship?

_____

_____

_____

3

THE FIRST PASSOVER
Exodus 12:1–51

DRAWING NEAR

Jewish people around the world today celebrate the festival of Passover to remind them of how God delivered their people from Egypt. What special celebrations do you and your family hold to remember God's goodness in the past?

_____

_____

_____

THE CONTEXT

The Lord had now sent nine plagues on Pharaoh, with each being more drastic than the last, yet Pharaoh had not relented. His heart was still hardened against God, and he would not permit the Israelites to leave. The Lord had consistently extended grace to the people of Egypt, but as we have discussed, the day of grace does eventually end. It was about to end for Egypt, for God was preparing to pour out His wrath.

The Lord commanded Moses and the Israelites to prepare for this calamitous event. Just as He had spared Israel from the devastating plagues, so He would now spare them from the most devastating of all: the death of every firstborn in the land. But this safety was not guaranteed, for the people were required to *do* something to protect themselves from the coming wrath. That protection would come in the form of blood—the blood of an innocent lamb—sprinkled on the doorposts of their houses.

The Lord told His people that when He saw the blood on the doorpost of a house, He would *pass over* that home and not inflict the plague. "Now the blood shall be a sign for you on the houses where you *are*. And when I see the blood, I will pass over you; and the plague shall not be on you to destroy you when I strike the land of Egypt" (Exodus 12:13). The Jewish people have celebrated the Passover feast around the world ever since this time.

In this study, we will learn where that feast originated and what its important symbols mean. Most importantly, we will discover the profundity of the sacrificial lamb, as it prefigures the greatest Lamb of all.

Keys to the Text

Read Exodus 12:1–51, noting the key words and phrases indicated below.

THE PASSOVER LAMB: The Lord commands Moses and the Israelites to commemorate their redemption from Egypt by sacrificing a lamb.

1. THE LORD SPOKE: Most likely, the instructions on the Passover were also given during the three days of darkness in order to fully prepare Israel for the grand finale, their Exodus from Egypt.

IN THE LAND: Later, when Israel was in the wilderness, Moses stated that the detailed instructions for this special feast day were not like those of the other special days, all of which had been given after the nation had left Egypt (see Exodus 23:14–17; Deuteronomy 16:1–8). The Passover was inextricably linked to what took place in the exodus, and that connection was never to be forgotten.

2. THE FIRST MONTH OF THE YEAR: The Lord instructed the Israelites to reestablish their calendar, with the new year beginning in the present month (March/April in the Western calendar). The Lord would later establish an annual feast day to commemorate this event. The Lord intended Passover to always be inextricably linked to Israel's redemption from Egypt. At the Last

Supper, Jesus commanded the disciples to begin keeping a similar observance, known today as Communion or the Lord's Table. This ordinance commemorates Christians' redemption from sin.

3. A LAMB: The Lord had not yet given Moses the Law, so the sacrificial system had not yet been established. But from the beginning the Lord demanded the sacrifice of an innocent lamb without blemish.

A LAMB FOR A HOUSEHOLD: Each household was commanded to obey the Lord's instructions in this matter. (In the same way today, each person must embrace the sacrifice of Christ for himself.) Those who refused to obey the Lord's command would face dire consequences.

4. TOO SMALL FOR THE LAMB: The Passover was to be available freely to all, with no household excluded. In the same way, the blood of Christ, which offers redemption from sin, is freely available to all who believe the gospel. No person is ineligible, and no sin is too great to be covered.

5. WITHOUT BLEMISH: The people were not to select a second-rate lamb for the sacrifice; only the very best would be acceptable. It was, in fact, to be *spotless*. Jesus was the only One who could pay the price for sin—the only *acceptable* sacrifice—because He was spotless and *without sin*. "You were not redeemed with corruptible things, like silver or gold, . . . but with the precious blood of Christ, as of a lamb without blemish and without spot" (1 Peter 1:18–19). "[God] made Him who knew no sin to be sin for us, that we might become the righteousness of God in Him" (2 Corinthians 5:21).

COVERED BY THE BLOOD: God instructs the Israelites to take the blood from the lamb and sprinkle it on their doors as an open sign that they belong to Him.

6. THE WHOLE ASSEMBLY OF THE CONGREGATION OF ISRAEL SHALL KILL IT: The entire nation of Israel—that is, every household—was responsible to slaughter a Passover lamb. In this way, each person was forced to recognize that the lamb was being slain for his or her own sin. It became a personal sacrifice.

AT TWILIGHT: According to Josephus, it was customary in his day to slaughter the lamb at around 3 PM. This was precisely the time of day when Christ, God's final Passover Lamb, died for our sins (see Luke 23:44–46).

7. ON THE TWO DOORPOSTS AND ON THE LINTEL: The Israelites were commanded to put the blood of the sacrifice on the doorposts and lintels of their houses (the top and two sides of the doorway). This was a bold and forthright sign that they were covered by the blood. Their sacrifice was not to be done in secret, but openly, letting the world know that they were obeying God's commands. Today, our Christian faith should be equally open and forthright, revealing for all to see that we are covered by the blood of the Lamb. "No one, when he has lit a lamp, puts it in a secret place or under a basket, but on a lampstand, that those who come in may see the light" (Luke 11:33).

THE PASSOVER MEAL: God tells the people that after sacrificing the lamb, they are to sit down to a meal—a very unique meal with a unique dress code.

8. WITH UNLEAVENED BREAD: Leaven is yeast, and it is often used in Scripture as a symbol of sin. A small amount of yeast affects the entire loaf of bread in the same way that the smallest sin makes a person unable to enter the presence of God. The Israelites were to eat bread without yeast to symbolize the fact that Christ, the final Lamb, would one day wash away people's sins completely, making them fit to enter God's presence.

AND WITH BITTER HERBS: The bitter herbs were a reminder to the people of the bitterness of their slavery in Egypt. Ironically, they would complain frequently once they were out of Egypt and suggest that their lives had been better there. This just shows how short human memory can be. We are to remember on a regular basis how helpless and hopeless we were before Christ redeemed us and how bitter life is without Him.

11. A BELT ON YOUR WAIST: The Passover was unique not only for its menu but also for its dress code. The Israelites would ordinarily not wear sandals at a meal, nor would they have a staff in hand. However, this meal was to be eaten in haste. Furthermore, the Lord commanded His people to eat the meal in clothes that implied a readiness to travel—they were to be *ready* at a moment's notice to get up and leave Egypt. Jesus likewise commanded His followers to be ready for His return: "Watch . . . for you do not know what hour your Lord is coming . . . If the master of the house had known what hour the thief would come, he would have watched and not allowed his house to be

broken into. Therefore you also be ready, for the Son of Man is coming at an hour you do not expect" (Matthew 24:42–44; see also Luke 12:39–41).

GOD'S JUDGMENT IS COMING: *The Lord now explains why this sacrifice is so vitally important: His judgment is about to fall on the Egyptians.*

11. THE LORD'S PASSOVER: This is where the name originated. The Lord's angel would pass through the nation of Egypt, striking down the first-born in each house. But the Lord's judgment would not fall on those who were covered in the blood of the Passover lamb. This is a powerful picture of Christ's sacrifice for our sins: the wrath of God will never fall on those who are covered in Christ's blood.

12. AGAINST ALL THE GODS OF EGYPT: The Lord had already demonstrated the utter powerlessness of Egypt's gods when He sent the previous nine plagues—many of which specifically mocked Egypt's pantheon. His final plague would now demonstrate in one fell swoop the utter folly of placing one's faith in anyone or anything but God Himself. The Lord was sending His angel throughout the nation, and there was no power on earth or in hell that could prevent His hand of judgment—no power, that is, except for the means of grace the Lord had outlined in the Passover stipulations.

13. WHEN I SEE THE BLOOD: This is a reminder that when the Lord looks on His children, He sees us through the blood of Christ, which covers our sins. On the other hand, a person whose sins are not covered by the blood of Christ is in imminent danger of God's judgment.

DO NOT FORGET: *The Lord commands the people of Israel to commemorate the Passover feast each year and to diligently teach their children what it means.*

14. A MEMORIAL: It is important for us as God's people to *remember* all He has done in our lives and, above all, to remember how He saved us and at what cost. "Then [Jesus] said to [His disciples], 'With fervent desire I have desired to eat this Passover with you before I suffer; for I say to you, I will no longer eat of it until it is fulfilled in the kingdom of God.' Then He took the

cup, and gave thanks, and said, 'Take this and divide it among yourselves; for I say to you, I will not drink of the fruit of the vine until the kingdom of God comes.' And He took bread, gave thanks and broke it, and gave it to them, saying, 'This is My body which is given for you; do this in remembrance of Me.' Likewise He also took the cup after supper, saying, 'This cup is the new covenant in My blood, which is shed for you'" (Luke 22:15–20).

15. REMOVE LEAVEN FROM YOUR HOUSES: Leaven symbolized sin, as stated previously, and the Lord commanded His people to cleanse their entire lives from it—even to the point of not having any in the house. Anyone who violated this command was to be cut off from Israel. The New Testament similarly commands us to remove the leaven from our own lives: "Therefore purge out the old leaven, that you may be a new lump, since you truly are unleavened. For indeed Christ, our Passover, was sacrificed for us" (1 Corinthians 5:7).

FOR WHOEVER EATS LEAVENED BREAD: We are further commanded to examine our lives for sin (leaven) prior to partaking of the Lord's Supper, or Communion. "As often as you eat this bread and drink this cup, you proclaim the Lord's death till He comes. Therefore whoever eats this bread or drinks this cup of the Lord in an unworthy manner will be guilty of the body and blood of the Lord. But let a man examine himself, and so let him eat of the bread and drink of the cup. For he who eats and drinks in an unworthy manner eats and drinks judgment to himself, not discerning the Lord's body. For this reason many are weak and sick among you, and many sleep. For if we would judge ourselves, we would not be judged" (1 Corinthians 11:26–31).

26. WHEN YOUR CHILDREN SAY TO YOU: The Lord instituted this Passover as a memorial feast to remind His children of what He had done to redeem them. Another vital way of remembering is to teach our children these things. The Scriptures are clear on this point: a father's duty includes teaching his children in the ways of the Lord. "Take heed to yourself, and diligently keep yourself, lest you forget the things your eyes have seen, and lest they depart from your heart all the days of your life. And teach them to your children and your grandchildren . . . the LORD said, 'Gather the people to Me, and I will let them hear My words, that they may learn to fear Me all the days they live on the earth, and that they may teach their children'" (Deuteronomy 4:9–10).

THE DESTROYER COMES: The Lord sends an angel throughout the land of Egypt, and not one household is spared—except the houses that are covered by the blood.

29. ALL THE FIRSTBORN IN THE LAND: God's final judgment on Pharaoh covered the entire land of Egypt. This same judgment of God will one day fall on all men with equal impartiality. Anyone who is not covered by the blood of Christ shall face God's righteous wrath—from the ruler of the land to the man who sits in the dungeon.

30. THERE WAS A GREAT CRY IN EGYPT: One shudders to imagine the horror of this dark night, as every household throughout Egypt arose in the middle hours to discover death. Yet this is just a small picture of the horror that awaits those who refuse to be covered by God's Passover Lamb. "But the sons of the kingdom will be cast out into outer darkness. There will be weeping and gnashing of teeth" (Matthew 8:12).

31. HE CALLED FOR MOSES AND AARON BY NIGHT: This is the reason the Lord commanded the people to eat the Passover feast in their traveling clothes, as their departure was imminent and sudden.

46. NOR SHALL YOU BREAK ONE OF ITS BONES: The Passover lamb shed its blood, but none of its bones were to be broken. This, too, prefigured Christ. "One of the soldiers pierced His side with a spear, and immediately blood and water came out . . . These things were done that the Scripture should be fulfilled, 'Not one of His bones shall be broken'" (John 19:34–36).

UNLEASHING THE TEXT

1) Why were the Israelites commanded to eat the Passover feast with a staff in their hand? With sandals on their feet? With a belt that hitched up their robes and kept them out of the way of their feet?

_____

_____

_____

2) List some of the items on the Passover menu. What did they symbolize? What is the spiritual equivalent of Passover for Christians?

_____

_____

_____

3) Why did the Lord command the blood of the Passover lamb be sprinkled around the door? What did this symbolize?

_____

_____

_____

4) Why did God's wrath fall on all the Egyptians in this manner? Why did He spare the Israelites?

_____

_____

_____

EXPLORING THE MEANING

The Passover lamb is a picture of Christ. On the night of the final plague, the Lord commanded His people to sacrifice an unblemished lamb and sprinkle the doorposts with its blood. The lamb was to be a young male, and it was to be cooked in fire rather than boiled. The sacrifice was to be made available to every household, and none were to be left wanting.

In these ways and many more, the Passover feast in general, and the sacrificial lamb in particular, present us with a detailed picture of the sacrifice of Christ. He is the holy, unblemished Lamb of God, and His death on the cross was the final sacrifice for sin. "The next day John saw Jesus coming toward him, and said, 'Behold! The Lamb of God who takes away the sin of the world!'" (John 1:29).

This truth is so important to God's people that we must guard against forgetting who paid for our sins and what that sacrifice cost Him.

God will never pour out His wrath on those who are covered in the blood. The Lord's wrath was about to fall on the Egyptians, and when it came, it fell indiscriminately on every household in Egypt—except for those that were sprinkled with the blood of the Passover lamb. That blood was an outward sign to the angel that everyone within the house belonged to God, and the angel was not permitted to touch them.

In the same way, Christians are sealed with the blood of Christ. We are eternally protected from God's wrath against sin, and no power can erase that seal. The destroying angel in Egypt did not look on individual people but on the blood—or the lack of it. When he saw the blood of the lamb, he passed by. When God looks on His people, He sees the precious blood of His Son, shed for us on the cross to pay the price for our sins. He does not pour out His judgment on us, for His judgment has *already* been poured out. That judgment fell on Christ, the final Passover Lamb.

Those who are not covered by the blood of Christ will face eternal judgment. The preceding principle has a corollary: those who are *not* covered by the blood of the Lamb will indeed face the wrath of God. The destroying angel went throughout the entire land of Egypt looking for the blood-sprinkled doorposts. He entered every single house that was not sprinkled with blood, slaying the firstborn.

There were no exceptions—even the cattle were not exempt. The Lord is no respecter of persons. He does not make special exceptions to this law for people who have lived good lives or given to the poor or observed strict religious rituals. There was only one thing that could prevent the destroyer from slaying the firstborn, and that was the blood of the Passover lamb. There is ultimately only one way to avoid the eternal wrath of God, and that is to be covered by the blood of Christ.

Christians are commanded to live in expectation of Christ's immediate return. The Israelites were commanded to eat the Passover feast dressed in an unusual fashion: with sandals and walking tunic and staff, ready to leap up and march forth at a moment's notice. This proved necessary that night, as Pharaoh drove them out of Egypt in the middle hours of darkness.

The Lord Jesus promised that He would return to take His people home, whisking us to heaven just as He suddenly carried His people out of Egypt. Christians are called to live expectantly, ever ready for the sudden and glorious appearing of Jesus Christ. We do not want to be found unprepared.

"But of that day and hour no one knows, not even the angels in heaven, nor the Son, but only the Father. Take heed, watch and pray; for you do not know when the time is. It is like a man going to a far country, who left his house and gave authority to his servants, and to each his work, and commanded the door-keeper to watch. Watch therefore, for you do not know when the master of the house is coming—in the evening, at midnight, at the crowing of the rooster, or in the morning—lest, coming suddenly, he find you sleeping. And what I say to you, I say to all: Watch!" (Mark 13:32–37).

REFLECTING ON THE TEXT

5) What might have happened if an Egyptian family had joined the Passover feast and sprinkled their doorposts with the lamb's blood? What does this suggest about God's grace?

_____

_____

_____

6) What would have happened if an Israelite family had not sprinkled the doorposts with the blood of the lamb? What does this suggest about God's justice?

_____

_____

7) In what ways does the Passover lamb symbolize the person and work of Christ?

_____

_____

_____

8) In what ways does God's judgment on Egypt foreshadow His coming judgment on the entire world? Why were the Israelites supposed to dress as if they were ready to leave at any moment? How should Christians be similarly prepared to leave this world at any moment?

_____

_____

_____

PERSONAL RESPONSE

9) Are you living with the expectancy of Christ's imminent return? How can you keep that expectation in mind this week?

_____

_____

_____

10) Are your sins covered by the sacrificial death of Jesus Christ? If not, what is preventing you from believing in Him?

_____

_____

_____

4

CROSSING THE RED SEA

Exodus 14:1–31

DRAWING NEAR

The Lord led the people of Israel to the shores of the Red Sea, where the Egyptian army could pursue them. Why do you think God leads His people into such situations?

_____

_____

_____

THE CONTEXT

The people of Israel had just left Egypt, carrying with them great wealth they had plundered from their former slave masters. They had witnessed unprecedented miracles that the Lord had done on their behalf, and they had seen the Egyptians plagued with great loss while they themselves remained unharmed. God had told them again and again that He planned to carry them out of bondage into the land of Canaan, and they had seen that the Lord's promises never fail.

But somehow all of this was quickly forgotten when they faced their first setback. They had not been traveling for more than a few days when they looked behind them to see Pharaoh's army in pursuit. This was the most powerful army in the world, and it is quite likely that Pharaoh had taken his most elite troops on this expedition. They were equipped with the best weapons of the day, including armed chariots—the equivalent of tanks in our time—and they were well trained and disciplined fighters. The Israelites, on the other hand, were newly released slaves who had never fought in combat and never wielded weapons.

From a human perspective, the Israelites were in deep trouble. Yet this human perspective is just what the Lord wants His people to avoid. He calls us to walk by faith, not by sight—to always be looking to God for assistance rather than to man or to ourselves. God had shown the people of Israel unequivocally that He would fight on their behalf, and He had proven beyond doubt that He would not abandon them. How quickly the people forgot those lessons when the enemy confronted them.

We can learn from the forgetfulness of the Israelites, because we are no different from them. It is vital that we remember what the Lord has done in our lives and to expect Him to work on our behalf in the future just as He has done in the past.

KEYS TO THE TEXT

Read Exodus 14:1–31, noting the key words and phrases indicated below.

> GOD'S PLAN EXPLAINED: *The Israelites have been released from Egypt, and God tells Moses to lead them toward the Red Sea. He has a plan to bring glory to His name in Egypt.*

1. THE LORD SPOKE TO MOSES: The Israelites had just left Egypt and were now heading into the desert region.

2. PI HAHIROTH, BETWEEN MIGDOL AND THE SEA, OPPOSITE BAAL ZEPHON: The exact locations of these sites are unknown. (See the map in the Introduction for possible routes the Israelites traveled during this time.)

BY THE SEA: That is, the Red Sea.

4. I WILL HARDEN PHARAOH'S HEART: As we discussed, this does not mean the Lord enticed Pharaoh to do evil, for Pharaoh had previously hardened himself against God. His moments of softening were temporary, and he still stubbornly remained set against the God of Israel. The Lord would permit

him to revert to his previous attitude toward Israel and use his stubborn wickedness for His glory.

I WILL GAIN HONOR: Man's wickedness does not frustrate God's plan for His people. He allows men and women to exercise their free will and decide for themselves whether to submit to Him—but He uses their actions, whether righteous or unrighteous, to bring glory to Himself.

THAT THE EGYPTIANS MAY KNOW THAT I AM THE LORD: God had chosen the descendants of Abraham to be His special people, set apart from the world around them. This was not for their personal gain but to show forth His glory and mercy to the entire world. He wanted the Egyptians to worship Him just as the Israelites did. He intervened in the affairs of Egypt in order to set His people free from bondage but also to show Himself to the Egyptians.

> ON SECOND THOUGHT: *After the Israelites are gone, the*
> *Egyptians wonder why they ever released them in the first place.*
> *Pharaoh goes out to bring them back.*

5. WHY HAVE WE DONE THIS? This response is almost humorous in its shortsightedness. The Egyptians had released the Israelites from slavery—indeed, they had driven them away—because the Lord's judgments were threatening to destroy their entire land. His final plague had killed the firstborn of every household! But once life began to settle back to normal, they forgot about the Lord's miraculous interventions and remembered only the huge profit they had enjoyed from the Hebrews' slave labor. This is a symptom of a heart that is hardened against God and refuses to acknowledge His miraculous displays of power and grace. The religious leaders in Israel would later take the same attitude toward Jesus, denying that His tremendous miracles of healing and raising the dead were displays of God's power—even attributing those miracles to the devil.

8. THE CHILDREN OF ISRAEL WENT OUT WITH BOLDNESS: At this point, the Israelites were trusting fully in the presence and power of God to protect them. It may have been easy to take such an attitude when the enemy was not close on their heels. Their faith would waver, unfortunately, when Pharaoh's army came into sight.

9. OVERTOOK THEM: Pharaoh's army could travel far more quickly in their chariots than the Israelites could on foot.

PANIC! The Israelites are filled with terror when they see Pharaoh's army bearing down on them.

10. THEY WERE VERY AFRAID: This is quite understandable from a human perspective, as Pharaoh's cavalry was the most powerful on earth at the time. It would be comparable to seeing an enemy nation rumbling toward you in tanks and armored vehicles.

CRIED OUT TO THE LORD: This was the proper response for the people to make in this situation. They had seen the Lord's unstoppable power in Egypt, and He had shown them repeatedly that He was their God and would not abandon them to their enemies. It would be reasonable to cry out to the Lord to intervene again and then trust Him to do so. Unfortunately, as the next verse reveals, their cry was one of anger.

11. WHY HAVE YOU SO DEALT WITH US: The Israelites responded to the very first threat in their travels by falsely accusing Moses—and ultimately, God—of treachery. The Lord had performed a great many miracles and wonders in Egypt that the whole nation had witnessed as demonstrations of God's presence and power. By openly voicing such false accusations against God, the Israelites were declaring to the world around them that they did not trust Him.

12. IT WOULD HAVE BEEN BETTER FOR US TO SERVE THE EGYPTIANS: This would become an almost constant refrain during the Israelites' travels. This lack of trust in God's faithfulness would eventually prevent this generation from entering the Promised Land, as we will see in a future study.

13. DO NOT BE AFRAID: The Lord frequently commands His people to take courage. On the one hand, fear is an emotion and as such is not easily controlled. But on the other hand, we actually breed fear in ourselves and in others by permitting it to take control. We overcome fear by focusing on the promises of God, remembering what He has done for us in the past, and by choosing to place our faith in Him rather than in the circumstances around us. The people had to choose whether to act in fear or in faith.

STAND STILL, AND SEE: In times of crisis, we can actually increase our own fear and anxiety by rushing about and trying to resolve the crisis. There are times when things are beyond our control, and in those situations the best response is to be still and see what the Lord will do on our behalf. "Be still, and know that I am God; I will be exalted among the nations, I will be exalted in the earth!" (Psalm 46:10).

14. THE LORD WILL FIGHT FOR YOU: The key to overcoming fear is to deliberately remind ourselves the all-powerful God is our champion. Hear the words of Paul: "What then shall we say to these things? If God is for us, who can be against us? He who did not spare His own Son, but delivered Him up for us all, how shall He not with Him also freely give us all things?" (Romans 8:31–32).

GOD'S PLAN UNFOLDS: The Lord tells Moses what to do with the people and then reiterates what He plans to do with the Egyptians. He intends to show everyone that He is God.

15. GO FORWARD: The Lord had begun a good work in the lives of the Israelites, and He would complete that work regardless of who attempted to prevent it. When people or circumstances conspire against us, our response should still be to *go forward* with the Lord, "being confident of this very thing, that He who has begun a good work in you will complete it until the day of Jesus Christ" (Philippians 1:6).

16. LIFT UP YOUR ROD, AND STRETCH OUT YOUR HAND: The Lord frequently commanded Moses or Aaron to do something prior to His working a great miracle. He did not need Moses' rod to part the Red Sea—there was no magical power in that rod, nor did Moses possess any special powers of his own. The Lord does not even need our obedience to accomplish His purposes. As we have seen, He can achieve His intentions even through the deliberate disobedience and rebellion of men. Nevertheless, He frequently calls us to some act of obedience in order to show the world that His people have faith in Him and that He is faithful and powerful to bring them safely through.

18. THE EGYPTIANS SHALL KNOW THAT I AM THE LORD: The Lord reiterated that His ultimate purpose in this miracle was not to destroy the Egyptians. Rather, it was to bring glory to His own name and to show the whole world that there is only one true God. It is important to remember that when the Lord works mightily on our behalf, His purpose is to bring His salvation to all people—even to our enemies.

GOD COMES BETWEEN: The Lord has been moving before Israel in a pillar of cloud and a pillar of fire. Now He moves the pillar between Israel and Pharaoh's army.

19. THE ANGEL OF GOD, WHO WENT BEFORE THE CAMP OF ISRAEL: The Lord was present in visible form to His people in a pillar of cloud by day

and a pillar of fire by night, moving in front of the vast horde as they traveled in the wilderness. In this case, however, He moved behind the Israelites in order to protect them.

20. IT CAME BETWEEN THE CAMP OF THE EGYPTIANS AND THE CAMP OF ISRAEL: The Lord intervened visibly between His people and their enemies, showing to both Israel and Egypt that He would not abandon His people.

IT WAS A CLOUD AND DARKNESS TO THE ONE: The Angel of the Lord, and the pillar of cloud and fire, moved from being the advance guard (leading the Israelites) to being the rear guard (protecting them from danger). The cloud created a blinding barrier between the camps of Israel and Egypt, making it impossible for the Egyptians to continue their pursuit until the cloud was lifted.

21. A STRONG EAST WIND ALL THAT NIGHT: The people did not need to do anything to accomplish their salvation. While they slept, the Lord worked a great miracle in front of them while also protecting them from the enemy behind them.

> GOD'S PLAN FULFILLED: *The Lord has miraculously intervened for His people once again, and all that remains is for the people to keep moving forward.*

22. THE CHILDREN OF ISRAEL WENT INTO THE MIDST OF THE SEA: This was an act of faith on the Israelites' part. It must have been daunting to walk between two huge walls of water, especially when they were not held in place by any visible force. The Lord had wrought a powerful miracle to deliver His people, but those people were still required to walk forward in faith. He did not carry them bodily across the Red Sea—their faith and obedience were required if they were to be saved from Pharaoh's army.

23. THE EGYPTIANS PURSUED: This was the ultimate military folly. One would think that by now Pharaoh would have recognized the power of God was inexorable and He would not fail to deliver His people. But Pharaoh had willfully blinded himself to the truth by hardening his heart and rejecting the Lord, and he was spiritually incapable of seeing the folly of riding his chariot between two great walls of water that might collapse on him at any moment.

25. LET US FLEE FROM THE FACE OF ISRAEL: Unfortunately, this realization of God's presence and power came too late for the Egyptians. As already stated, the day of God's grace does not last forever. Those who have steadfastly rejected Him may one day find that they have lost the opportunity to repent.

29. THE CHILDREN OF ISRAEL HAD WALKED ON DRY LAND: The Lord used the same force both to deliver His children and to destroy their enemies.

31. THE PEOPLE FEARED THE LORD, AND BELIEVED THE LORD: When the Lord effects a miracle in our lives, it is important to make an effort to remember that event. The people of Israel would quickly forget the Lord's great deliverance at the Red Sea, even as they had forgotten His great intervention to free them from bondage. Our human nature makes it easy for us to forget God's faithfulness when circumstances are against us—even if we were praising Him just a day before.

UNLEASHING THE TEXT

1) Why were the Israelites so afraid when they saw Pharaoh's army? How would you have responded in that situation?

_____

_____

_____

2) If you had been in the Israelite camp, how would you have felt when the pillar of cloud moved between you and the Egyptians? How well would you have slept that night?

_____

_____

_____

_____

3) How do you think the people of Israel felt as they walked through the Red Sea between great walls of water? When they saw Pharaoh's army destroyed?

_____

_____

_____

4) Why do you think Pharaoh and his people changed their minds about letting the Israelites go?

_____

_____

_____

EXPLORING THE MEANING

Do not forget what the Lord has done. The people of Israel had seen many amazing miracles when the Lord had demonstrated His power and His determination to set them free from slavery. God had sent ten plagues that devastated Egypt but left the Israelites unharmed. He had spoken to them through Moses, predicting that Pharaoh would drive them out of Egypt, heavily laden with gold and silver—and it had happened exactly as promised. Yet when the first setback occurred, they instantly forgot all those signs and wonders and accused God of betraying them.

This is a characteristic common to all humans—indeed, it is part of our nature. We rejoice when the Lord blesses us and give Him glory and thanks for His loving intervention in our lives. But then something goes wrong—some unexpected threat arises—and we are immediately filled with fear and doubt. We wonder if the Lord has abandoned us, or we forget to trust Him and rely instead on our own power to solve the matter.

It is vital for us to remember what the Lord has done in our lives so we don't become fearful when circumstances go against us. If the Lord was faithful in the past, we can be confident that He will be faithful in the future. "Beware that you do not forget the Lord your God by not keeping His commandments, His judgments, and His statutes which I command you today" (Deuteronomy 8:11). "Bless the LORD, O my soul, and forget not all His benefits" (Psalm 103:2).

Do not fear what men may do to you. Pharaoh was the most powerful man in the most powerful nation on earth. His army was feared around the known world, and they were equipped with the latest technologies and the best training. The Israelites, on the other hand, were newly released slaves with no military experience and no chariots. It is no wonder that they were frightened when they looked behind them and saw the great dust cloud of Pharaoh's army bearing down.

But the greatest army on earth is no match for the power of God. The Lord led the Egyptians into the Red Sea and then plucked off the wheels of their chariots as simply as a man snaps a toothpick. At the same time, He led His people through the sea on dry ground. They did not even get their feet wet!

Our tendency is to focus on what we can see and to believe the evidence of our senses. But the Lord calls us to walk by faith, not by sight, and to rely fully on His unlimited power and faithfulness. "In God I have put my trust; I will not be afraid. What can man do to me?" (Psalm 56:11). "For He Himself has said, 'I will never leave you nor forsake you.' So we may boldly say: 'The Lord is my helper; I will not fear. What can man do to me?'" (Hebrews 13:5–6).

If we harden our heart, we will become blind to the truth. Pharaoh stubbornly refused to believe the Lord was the one true God, and he repeatedly hardened his heart against God's attempts to bring him into submission. Each time Moses warned him that a plague was coming—predicting when it would start, what it would do, and even how its damage could be lessened—Pharaoh still would not relent. Even after the Lord had sent horrible devastation on his land, including the death of all firstborns, he could not see what should have been obvious: he could not defeat the power of God.

As mentioned in the previous principle, it is in our human nature to place our faith in the evidence of our senses—but our eyes cannot always discern the truth of God. We must exercise faith to discern the truth of God, and we must place that faith in the Word of God and in His holy character. When we reject God's Word, we willfully blind ourselves to the truth. A person with a hardened heart will walk about like a blind man, stumbling into trouble and falling into pits.

"Oh come, let us worship and bow down; let us kneel before the LORD our Maker. For He is our God, and we are the people of His pasture, and the sheep of His hand. Today, if you will hear His voice: 'Do not harden your hearts, as in the rebellion, as in the day of trial in the wilderness, when your fathers tested Me; they tried Me, though they saw My work'" (Psalm 95:6–9). Today is the day to listen to God's voice.

REFLECTING ON THE TEXT

5) What were the people implying about God's character when they accused Him of leading them into the wilderness to destroy them?

_____

_____

_____

6) What were the Lord's purposes in doing the miracles in this chapter of Exodus? What does this teach us about His character?

_____

_____

_____

7) Why did the people of Israel accuse God of betraying them? How would you have responded in their situation?

_____

_____

_____

8) When have you been afraid of what other people could do to you? How did the Lord show His power on your behalf?

_____

_____

_____

PERSONAL RESPONSE

9) Have you hardened your heart toward God? If so, what will you do this week to soften your heart?

_____

_____

_____

10) When have you been encouraged by remembering what the Lord has done in your life? When have you become discouraged or afraid because you forgot?

_____

_____

_____

5

THE LAW OF GOD
Exodus 20:1–21

DRAWING NEAR

How would you define the purpose of laws in a society? How are manmade laws different from God's laws?

_____

_____

_____

THE CONTEXT

After the Israelites miraculously crossed through the Red Sea, the Lord led them into the wilderness and guided them toward Mount Sinai. It was exactly three months to the day from their departure from Egypt when they reached Sinai and camped at its base. There the Lord made His presence known with dramatic signs: terrible thunder and lightning, the noise of loud trumpet blasts, and a thick smoke rising up and engulfing the mountain. He forbade the people to set foot on the mountain or even to approach it, for He was there and His holiness would not permit the presence of sin.

The people were filled with fear. They recognized they were in the presence of a holy God, and they were convicted of their sinful state. What hope would they have of ever knowing God? Yet God invited Moses up onto the mountain, and there gave him a series of commandments by which the people were to live. Through His Law, God's people were given a means of access into His presence—a distant and incomplete access, but a means of knowing Him all the same.

The entire Law was detailed and long—much too long for a single study such as this. But on this occasion, the Lord gave Moses a sort of summary in the form of the Ten Commandments. These commandments encapsulated the entire law and teach us today, just as they did for the Israelites, what it means to follow God's moral law. As we will see in this study, Jesus and the New Testament writers often referred back to the Ten Commandments. In fact, Jesus summarized all the law with the two greatest commandments: love God with all your heart, and love your neighbor as yourself.

KEYS TO THE TEXT

Read Exodus 20:1–21, noting the key words and phrases indicated below.

GOD SPEAKS: *The Israelites reach Mount Sinai just three months after the exodus from Egypt. Moses ascends the mountain, and there the Lord gives him the Ten Commandments.*

1. GOD SPOKE: The Israelites were now encamped at the base of Mount Sinai, and the Lord had called Moses to ascend the mountain so He could speak to him. The teachings He gave, known as the Ten Commandments, briefly summarized what the Lord expected of His people. The actual Law that God gave to Moses was far more detailed, listing many different sacrifices and worship practices as well as specifics on forbidden actions and their consequences.

2. I AM THE LORD: The word translated LORD in the Old Testament (often printed in small capitals, as in the *New King James Version*) is translated *Jehovah*, meaning "the existing one." The name is also sometimes spelled *Yahweh*.

IDOLATRY: *The Lord's first commandment is the most detailed. God's people are to worship Him and Him alone.*

3. NO OTHER GODS BEFORE ME: This does not mean God's people are permitted to have other gods, so long as they are of less importance than the

Lord. It literally means, "You shall have no other gods *in My face;* no other gods in my presence." All false gods stand in opposition to the true God, and the worship of them is incompatible with the worship of Yahweh. God's people are to worship and serve Him alone, and they are to take care not to allow anything else become a false god in their lives.

4. CARVED IMAGE: The people of Moses' day frequently made statues of animals or mythical gods to whom they prayed and worshiped. The Israelites themselves would soon make a golden calf, even as Moses was on the mountain speaking with God! However, here God was saying the mode of worship appropriate to Him forbids any attempt to represent or caricature Him by use of anything He had made. Total censure of artistic expression was not the issue, but the absolute censure of idolatry and false worship. It is in our sinful human nature to desire a god that can be seen and handled, but God calls His people to walk by faith rather than by sight (see 2 Corinthians 5:7).

5. BOW DOWN TO THEM NOR SERVE THEM: Bowing before something indicates a person is submitting himself to that idol's authority. Serving involves labor and using the work of one's hands to please an idol or to further an idol's goals. Many things can become idols in our lives—not just carved images of bulls or fish. We risk making anything an idol when we give it authority in our lives, or allow something to determine our daily schedule, or make something a top financial priority.

A JEALOUS GOD: This sense of jealousy is akin to the protective jealousy a man has toward his wife—his resentment of any attempt to woo her away from him. The Lord is passionately protective of His people, and His anger burns toward anyone or anything that tries to draw away their worship.

VISITING THE INIQUITY OF THE FATHERS UPON THE CHILDREN: This does not mean children are punished for their parents' sins, which, in fact, is forbidden according to God's Law (see Deuteronomy 24:16). Rather, it means the sin of idolatry will affect a person's children for several generations. A man who worships something besides the one true God will pass on that idolatry to his children, and God's judgment will also last for several generations. The difference in consequence served as both a warning and a motivation. The effect of a disobedient generation was to plant wickedness so deeply that it took several generations to reverse.

THOSE WHO HATE ME: The Lord made a black-and-white distinction here: anyone who does not worship Him—anyone who allows an idol to take precedence in his life—hates God. "No one can serve two masters," Jesus later confirmed, "for either he will hate the one and love the other, or else he will be loyal to the one and despise the other. You cannot serve God and mammon" (Matthew 6:24).

6. THOUSANDS: God's judgment would fall on idolaters to the third and fourth generation, but His mercy would be lavished on thousands. This under-scores that God's mercy is far greater and far more frequent than His wrath.

SWEARING AND SABBATH: The Lord warns His people against taking false oaths, which brings discredit to His name. He also reminds them to rest on the seventh day.

7. TAKE THE NAME OF THE LORD YOUR GOD IN VAIN: The Lord had revealed His name to Moses, and He would soon reveal His glory. These gifts, however, brought responsibility to God's people. We are permitted to know His name, but we are equally forbidden to abuse that name. Such abuse includes anything that will bring disrepute to His character, such as making false claims or promises. "You have heard that it was said to those of old, 'You shall not swear falsely, but shall perform your oaths to the Lord.' But I say to you, do not swear at all . . . let your 'Yes' be 'Yes,' and your 'No,' 'No.' For whatever is more than these is from the evil one" (Matthew 5:33–34, 37).

8. REMEMBER THE SABBATH DAY: The term *Sabbath* is derived from the idea "to rest or cease from work." Each seventh day belonged to the Lord and would not be a workday, but one set apart (made holy) for rest and for time devoted to the worship of Yahweh. The Lord created the entire universe, including mankind, in six literal twenty-four-hour days, and He rested on the seventh day. He then "blessed the Sabbath day and hallowed it," meaning He added a special blessing into His laws of creation for those who followed His example by resting on the seventh day.

10. ON IT YOU SHALL NOT DO ANY WORK: Jesus would later warn against legalistic observation of the Law, including this Sabbath law. "The Sabbath was made for man, and not man for the Sabbath" (Mark 2:27). Sig-nificantly, the command to observe the Sabbath is not repeated in the New Testament, whereas the other nine of the Ten Commandments are. In fact, it is clearly nullified (see Colossians 2:16–17), meaning it is no longer binding for God's people. Because it was specifically intended for Israel during the Mosaic

economy, the Sabbath mandate does not directly apply to believers today (who are part of the church age).

HONOR YOUR PARENTS: This is the first command that brings with it a positive promise: "Honor your parents and you will live a long life."

12. HONOR YOUR FATHER AND YOUR MOTHER: To *honor* means to esteem highly, to respect. It includes the elements of obeying our parents when we are young and caring for them when they are old. The key to societal stability is reverence and respect for parents and their authority.

THAT YOUR DAYS MAY BE LONG: The appended promise primarily related the command to life in the Promised Land and reminded the Israelites of the program God had set up for Him and his people. Within the borders of the Israelites' territory, God expected them not to tolerate juvenile delinquency, which at heart is overt disrespect for parents and authority. Severe consequences—namely, capital punishment—could apply. In the New Testament, Paul echoed this teaching of the Law, quoting from the book of Deuteronomy: "Children, obey your parents in the Lord, for this is right. 'Honor your father and mother,' which is the first commandment with promise: 'that it may be well with you and you may live long on the earth'" (Ephesians 6:1–3).

GETTING ALONG WITH OTHERS: The following commandments teach us how to live in peace with our neighbors.

13. MURDER: The irreversible nature of the divinely imposed sentence of death on every manslayer who killed another intentionally stands without parallel in ancient Near Eastern literature and legal codes. Jesus would remind people of this law and teach them undue anger is no better: "You have heard that it was said to those of old, 'You shall not murder, and whoever murders will be in danger of the judgment.' But I say to you that whoever is angry with his brother without a cause shall be in danger of the judgment" (Matthew 5:21–22). Later, John wrote, "Whoever hates his brother is a murderer, and you know that no murderer has eternal life abiding in him" (1 John 3:15).

14. ADULTERY: This command, which was applicable to both men and women, protected the sacredness of the marriage relationship. Jesus took this

commandment seriously and taught that lust in the heart was equal to adultery in the body (in terms of its culpability before God). "You have heard that it was said to those of old, 'You shall not commit adultery.' But I say to you that whoever looks at a woman to lust for her has already committed adultery with her in his heart" (Matthew 5:27–28).

15. STEAL: Any dishonest acquiring of another's goods or assets greatly disturbs the right to ownership of private property, which is an important principle for societal stability. Nothing changed with regard to theft between the old covenant and the new. "Let him who stole steal no longer," Paul wrote, "but rather let him labor, working with his hands what is good, that he may have something to give him who has need" (Ephesians 4:28).

16. FALSE WITNESS: Justice is never served by untruthful testimony. Jesus taught the penchant to lie against one's neighbor comes straight from man's heart—and defiles him. "But those things which proceed out of the mouth come from the heart, and they defile a man. For out of the heart proceed evil thoughts, murders, adulteries, fornications, thefts, false witness, blasphemies" (Matthew 15:18–19).

17. COVET: The thoughts and desires of the heart do not escape God's attention—a strong longing to have what another has is wrong. "Where do wars and fights come from among you?" wrote James, the brother of Christ. "Do they not come from your desires for pleasure that war in your members? You lust and do not have. You murder and covet and cannot obtain. You fight and war. Yet you do not have because you do not ask. You ask and do not receive, because you ask amiss, that you may spend it on your pleasures" (James 4:1–3). Coveting gets us nowhere.

GOD'S TERRIFYING PRESENCE: The Lord next reminds His people that they should not take lightly their privilege of entering His presence.

18. THUNDERINGS: The Lord made His presence known through powerful symbols, both audible and visible (see Exodus 19:16). The people witnessed terrific thunderclaps and lightning flashes, terrifying trumpet blasts, and a thick smoke that engulfed the top of Mount Sinai. The presence of God is a frightening thing to sinful men and women. Christians can enter His presence boldly and with confidence only because we are covered by the blood of the

Lamb, His Son Jesus Christ. Without Christ, God's presence would be terrible and deadly.

19. LET NOT GOD SPEAK WITH US, LEST WE DIE: This was not because the Lord was angry with the people but simply because He was holy and they were not. Again, the Christian's access to the Father is made possible only by the propitiation of His Son. Prior to Christ, no man but the high priest could enter His presence and live, and that occurred only once a year according to rigorous stipulations.

20. SO THAT YOU MAY NOT SIN: It is purifying to be reminded of the awe-inspiring holiness and power of God. It can be easy for Christians to take God's goodness for granted, indulging in sinful behavior and expecting a "cheap grace." But Paul warned about this very inclination: "What shall we say then? Shall we continue in sin that grace may abound? Certainly not! How shall we who died to sin live any longer in it?" (Romans 6:1–2).

UNLEASHING THE TEXT

1) Review the Ten Commandments and put each into your own words. What practical examples of each can you give from your own life?

_____

_____

_____

_____

2) What does it mean to honor one's parents? How is that done as an adult?

_____

_____

_____

_____

3) What does it mean to *covet?* Give practical examples from modern life.

_____

_____

_____

4) Why did Jesus say that lusting after another person is the same as committing adultery? Or that hating another person is the same as committing murder in one's heart? What implications does this teaching hold for your life?

_____

_____

_____

_____

EXPLORING THE MEANING

Living by the Ten Commandments will not bring eternal life. The Lord gave His people the Law to show them what He expected of His children and to provide a temporary measure of sacrifice for sins. But the Law could not save anyone, because animal sacrifices and behavioral rules cannot change the heart or make final atonement for sin. Only the blood of Christ, God's perfect sacrificial Lamb, can provide forgiveness for man's sin and reconciliation with a holy God.

Paul taught that the Law was given to God's people to make them fully aware of their sinful state—to demonstrate that it was impossible to enter the presence of a holy God simply because they could never be holy in and of themselves. Sin is a part of our nature that cannot be erased by good deeds. In fact, it is impossible for fallen men and women to keep God's law perfectly.

"What purpose then does the law serve? It was added because of transgressions, till the Seed should come to whom the promise was made . . . If there had been a law given which could have given life, truly righteousness would have been by the law. But the Scripture has confined all under sin, that the promise by faith in Jesus Christ might be given to those who believe. But before faith came, we were kept under guard by the law, kept for the faith which would afterward be revealed. Therefore the law was our tutor to bring us to Christ, that we might be justified by faith. But after faith has come, we are no longer under a tutor" (Galatians 3:19, 21–25).

The Ten Commandments are still valid for Christians today. God gave the Law as a temporary measure to enable His people to enter His presence and live in obedience to His will. The death and resurrection of Christ represented the final atonement for sin, and it is only through faith in Christ that anyone can find peace with God. Nevertheless, the Ten Commandments (with the exception of the Sabbath) still present principles of godliness that the Lord expects of His people today.

The many New Testament passages we have just quoted demonstrate this. Jesus came to fulfill the Law by providing free access into the presence of God through His final sacrifice, and He gave us His Holy Spirit to enable us to fulfill the principles of godliness—the principles outlined in the Ten Commandments—in our own lives. Those principles of godly behavior are as important today as they were in Moses' day.

"Do not think that I came to destroy the Law or the Prophets," Christ Himself said. "I did not come to destroy but to fulfill. For assuredly, I say to you, till heaven and earth pass away, one jot or one tittle will by no means pass from the law till all is fulfilled. Whoever therefore breaks one of the least of these commandments, and teaches men so, shall be called least in the kingdom of heaven; but whoever does and teaches them, he shall be called great in the kingdom of heaven" (Matthew 5:17–19).

All of God's Law is summarized by the two greatest commandments. A young man once asked Jesus, "Teacher, which is the great commandment in the law?" Jesus answered, "'You shall love the Lord your God with all your heart, with all your soul, and with all your mind.' This is the first and great commandment. And the second is like it: 'You shall love your neighbor as yourself.' On these two commandments hang all the Law and the Prophets" (Matthew 22:36–40).

The Ten Commandments fall into these two categories. Some of them spell out what it means to love God with all our hearts, souls, and minds, while others give practical ways of loving our neighbors as ourselves. Together, these two principles summarize what it means to live a godly life.

"For the commandments, 'You shall not commit adultery,' 'You shall not murder,' 'You shall not steal,' 'You shall not bear false witness,' 'You shall not covet,' and if there is any other commandment, are all summed up in this saying, namely, 'You shall love your neighbor as yourself.' Love does no harm to a neighbor; therefore love is the fulfillment of the law" (Romans 13:9–10).

REFLECTING ON THE TEXT

5) Review the Ten Commandments and place them into these two
   categories:

   Love God with all your heart

   _____

   _____

   _____

   Love your neighbor as yourself

   _____

   _____

   _____

6) Which of the commandments do you struggle to obey? Which do you
   find fairly easy to do? Why do you think this is the case?

   _____

   _____

   _____

7) What does it mean to "love the Lord your God with all your heart, with all your soul, and with all your mind" (Matthew 22:37)? What is involved in this?

_____

_____

_____

8) What does it mean to love your neighbor as yourself? How does this compare with the culture's emphasis on self-esteem and self-fulfillment?

_____

_____

_____

PERSONAL RESPONSE

9) Which of the Ten Commandments convicts you of sin? How might the Lord be leading you to change this week?

_____

_____

_____

10) Are you living by the two greatest commandments? How can you deepen your love of God? How can you deepen your love for others?

_____

_____

_____

6

MOSES ON THE MOUNTAIN

Exodus 33:1–34:35

DRAWING NEAR

What are some instances in your life when fear got the better of you and you made some decisions you later regretted?

_____

_____

_____

THE CONTEXT

The Lord had been traveling with His people in the desert, going before them and behind them in a pillar of cloud by day and a pillar of fire by night. He had revealed to them many things about His character and what He expected of them. He had also begun to outline the law that He would give to them through Moses.

However, when Moses delayed coming down from Mount Sinai, the people began to fear he had perished. They said to Aaron, "This Moses . . . we do not know what has become of him" (Exodus 32:1). In their panic and impatience, they succumbed to a pagan worldview and fashioned a golden calf to worship. After they had committed this sin, the Lord said to Moses, "Go, get down! For your people whom you brought out of the land of Egypt have corrupted themselves" (verse 7). God threatened judgment against the Israelites, but He relented when Moses interceded on their behalf.

The actions of the people emphasized the fact that a gulf of separation existed between the two sides. As we will see in the next study, the Lord would soon give the people instructions concerning the construction of a portable tabernacle (literally "dwelling place"), and all the details of that tabernacle would also accentuate the reality of this gulf of separation. A holy God simply could not permit a sinful mankind to enter into His presence, and no one could look on His face and survive.

In spite of this, God still remained present with His people. He was with them in the pillars of cloud and fire, and He would be with them in His tabernacle. He would also be with His servant Moses. He would speak with Moses "face to face," as one friend speaks to another, and reveal His glory to him. This was the relationship Moses had with God, and it is similar to the relationship Christians freely enjoy today with the Lord through the blood of Jesus Christ.

KEYS TO THE TEXT

Read Exodus 33:1–34:35, noting the key words and phrases indicated below.

> GOOD NEWS AND BAD NEWS: *In spite of the people's sin, the Lord will allow them to continue on to the Promised Land. But there will be a consequence for their actions.*

3. I WILL NOT GO UP IN YOUR MIDST: God would not forfeit the people's entrance into the Promised Land, but He would withdraw His presence on the way. While the Lord's sworn covenant promise to the patriarchs could not be broken, His divine presence could be set aside because of sin.

4. THEY MOURNED, AND NO ONE PUT ON HIS ORNAMENTS: The removal of the people's jewelry outwardly depicted the sorrow of their hearts. It was a response similar to donning sackcloth and ashes.

> SPEAKING WITH GOD: *The Lord's presence traveled with the Israelites in a pillar of cloud or of fire, and Moses spoke with Him face to face.*

7. THE TABERNACLE OF MEETING: The Lord had given the Israelites specific instructions on how to make a portable tabernacle for use during the

exodus from Egypt (see Exodus 25). Before this tabernacle was constructed, the people would seek the Lord at Moses' tent. There, Moses would talk "face to face" with God.

9. THE PILLAR OF CLOUD: The Angel of the Lord traveled with God's people during their exodus and wilderness wanderings in a pillar of cloud during the day and a pillar of fire at night. The cloud shielded the people from the sun, while the fire provided light in the darkness. Each provided a visible manifestation of the Lord to guide the people and remind them of His presence.

11. FACE TO FACE: As we will see in this chapter, the Lord did not literally show His face to Moses. Nevertheless, He spoke with Moses intimately and audibly, as two men might speak together in private.

AS A MAN SPEAKS TO HIS FRIEND: Abraham was called "a friend of God" (James 2:23), and Moses also shared an intimacy with the Lord that is enjoyed by close friends. Christians are also called God's friends. As Jesus said, "You are My friends if you do whatever I command you. No longer do I call you servants, for a servant does not know what his master is doing; but I have called you friends, for all things that I heard from My Father I have made known to you" (John 15:14–15).

12. I KNOW YOU BY NAME: God's friendship is no mere acquaintance—He knows His people intimately. "The very hairs of your head are all numbered" (Luke 12:7).

A GODLY LEADER: Moses demonstrates several important aspects of godly leadership as he interacts with the Lord.

13. SHOW ME NOW YOUR WAY: The Lord had called Moses to lead a vast horde of people through the wilderness to the Promised Land, but Moses recognized his own limitations. He felt inadequate for the task and asked the Lord to give him wisdom and knowledge. This is the mark of a godly leader: to recognize one's strength is insufficient and to completely rely on God for wisdom and knowledge.

CONSIDER THAT THIS NATION IS YOUR PEOPLE: Moses interceded regularly for those under his leadership. On several occasions the Lord's anger burned against the people, but Moses interceded on their behalf and the Lord stayed His hand of judgment. This is another mark of a godly leader: to pray regularly for those under one's authority.

16. HOW THEN WILL IT BE KNOWN: Moses also was concerned about the people's witness to the world around them. If the Lord's presence was not obvious to the world, Moses reasoned, then His people would not be any different from the world. This, too, is a mark of a godly leader: to be jealous of the Lord's reputation, ensuring that one's own life and ministry are bearing a good witness of the Lord's presence.

SHOW ME YOUR GLORY: Moses makes an amazingly bold request of the Lord by asking to see His glory. But no man may see God's face and live.

18. SHOW ME YOUR GLORY: The Lord had already revealed His glory to some extent through the pillars of cloud and fire, and He had made known His unlimited power through the plagues He had sent on Egypt and the miracles He had provided to His people. He met with Moses regularly and spoke to him as a friend—yet Moses wanted more! What is perhaps even more amazing is the fact that God was not displeased with the request. The Lord wants His children to hunger for deeper intimacy with Him and to yearn to know Him more truly and profoundly than they already do.

19. ALL MY GOODNESS: The Lord revealed His character to Moses, showing him still more of His goodness, mercy, justice, and grace. This is a mystery: we are not told specifically what Moses saw, nor can we conceive how human eyes could perceive the full goodness of God.

THE NAME OF THE LORD: A person's name was thought to embody his character and describe his true nature. The name of the Lord is the expression of His nature, encapsulating who He is—"I am who I am" (Exodus 3:14).

I WILL BE GRACIOUS TO WHOM I WILL BE GRACIOUS: This does not mean that the Lord is capricious and shows grace in an arbitrary manner. Rather, it means that He is absolutely sovereign and orders the affairs of mankind as He sees fit. If He chooses to bestow His grace on a person, nothing can prevent it.

20. YOU CANNOT SEE MY FACE: Sinful man cannot enter the holy presence of God. Adam once walked with God, speaking to Him face to face, but after he sinned, he was cast out of God's presence. Through the blood of Christ, however, our fellowship with God is restored, "for through Him we . . . have access by one Spirit to the Father" (Ephesians 2:18). In eternity, God's people shall see Him face to face.

22. I WILL PUT YOU IN THE CLEFT OF THE ROCK: God enabled Moses to see some of His glory by protecting Him in the "cleft of the rock." In the same way, God enables Christians to see His face because we are protected by the Rock of Ages, bathed in the blood of Jesus Christ.

RENEWING THE COVENANT: The Lord instructs Moses to again ascend Mount Sinai, where He will renew the covenant between Himself and the people.

34:1 CUT TWO TABLETS OF STONE: Renewal of the covenant meant replacing the original broken tablets on which God had personally written the Ten Commandments.

4. WENT UP MOUNT SINAI: Mount Sinai was the place where the Lord had met with Moses and given him the original Ten Commandments (see the map in the Introduction). After the people sinned by worshiping the golden calf (see Exodus 32), Moses depicted the nation breaking God's commandments by actually breaking the tablets on which they were written.

6–7. THE LORD, THE LORD GOD: In these verses the Lord provides testimony of His character.

12. TAKE HEED TO YOURSELF, LEST YOU MAKE A COVENANT: International diplomacy, with its parity or suzerainty treaties, was not an option for Israel in dealing with the tribes living within the designated borders of the Promised Land. These treaties were accompanied by the names of the nations' gods, so it was fitting to deliver a charge not to make a treaty (covenant) with them, nor to serve their pagan gods.

LEST IT BE A SNARE: The Lord warned how idolatry could easily ensnare the people, by seemingly innocent invitations to join the festivities like a good neighbor or by intermarriage, because these events would require recognition of the contracting parties' deities. The Israelites' future history demonstrated the urgency of such instruction and the disaster of disobeying it.

20. ALL THE FIRSTBORN OF YOUR SONS YOU SHALL REDEEM: Back in Egypt, the firstborn of Israel—both man and animal—had been untouched by the tenth plague, so it was fitting for them to be set aside as special to God.

23. THREE TIMES IN THE YEAR ALL YOUR MEN SHALL APPEAR BEFORE THE LORD: God's requirement for all Israelite males to be present at three specified feasts would have had a socially and religiously uniting effect on

the nation. The men had to trust the Lord to protect their landholdings while on pilgrimage to the tabernacle. All three feasts were joyful occasions, being a commemoration of the exodus (the Feast of Unleavened Bread), an expression of gratitude to God for the grain He had provided (the Feast of Harvest), and a thanksgiving for the final harvest (the Feast of Ingathering).

MOSES WEARS A VEIL: When Moses comes down from Mount Sinai after meeting with God, his face glows with the Lord's reflected glory.

29. THE TWO TABLETS OF THE TESTIMONY: The second set of stone tablets on which the Ten Commandments were written.

THE SKIN OF HIS FACE SHONE: Moses' face glowed with a reflection of God's glory because he had been in the presence of the Lord, speaking to him "face to face." Similarly, the people with whom we interact will discern we have been in the presence of the Lord when they see the fruit of His Spirit displayed in our actions and attitudes (see 2 Corinthians 3:7–17).

30. THEY WERE AFRAID TO COME NEAR HIM: The holiness of God is so unapproachable to sinful men that even a mere reflection of it is terrifying. Jesus called His followers "the light of the world" (Matthew 5:14) and instructed them to reflect His light to the lost. It can be both compelling and frightening when others see the light of Christ's holiness reflected in our lives.

33. HE PUT A VEIL ON HIS FACE: The Holiest of Holies was the place within the tabernacle where the high priest met with God annually. The Ark of the Covenant, which represented the presence of God, was kept there. This section was separated from the rest of the tabernacle by a heavy veil to prevent anyone from entering the presence of God—for to do so meant certain death. But when Jesus died on the cross, that veil was miraculously torn apart from top to bottom, indicating that Christians now have access directly to the Father through the death of Christ.

34. HE WOULD TAKE THE VEIL OFF UNTIL HE CAME OUT: Moses veiled his face whenever he was not speaking to the Lord or authoritatively on His behalf. Paul wrote that though "the children of Israel could not look steadily at the face of Moses because of the glory of his countenance," that reflection of God's glory "was passing away" (2 Corinthians 3:7). The shining countenance was a mere reflection of God's glory, not of any glory within Moses himself,

and it faded when he was not in the presence of the Lord. Although our faces do not literally glow, the glory of God is also reflected through the lives of His children today. Because we have the Holy Spirit Himself dwelling within us, that reflection does not fade away.

UNLEASHING THE TEXT

1) List some of the ways God showed His glory to the people of Israel. What did these things reveal about His character?

_____

_____

_____

2) What is meant by "God's glory"? When have you seen some of God's glory in your own life?

_____

_____

_____

3) Why were the people afraid of Moses' glowing face? Why did he need a veil?

_____

_____

_____

4) Whom do you know who reflects the glory of God in his or her life? What aspect of His glory is reflected? What about in your life?

_____

_____

_____

Exploring the Meaning

The Lord wants His children to draw closer to Him. Moses made an audacious request of God when he asked to see His glory. After all, the Lord was already showing His presence among His people in many astonishing ways, including miracles and power and glory. Yet Moses yearned to know more about God, and the Lord was pleased to grant him as much as he was able to bear.

In the same way, the Lord has already revealed much of His glory to His people today by redeeming them from sin and making His presence freely available to all Christians. Yet there is so much more to know! We can deepen our understanding of His character through diligently reading and studying the Bible and by humbly asking Him to teach us more about Himself.

"All Scripture is given by inspiration of God, and is profitable for doctrine, for reproof, for correction, for instruction in righteousness, that the man of God may be complete, thoroughly equipped for every good work" (2 Timothy 3:16–17). "Draw near to God and He will draw near to you" (James 4:8).

We were once separated from God's presence, but Christ has given us free access. Moses veiled his face because the Israelites could not bear to look on the glow of God's glory—even though it was just a fading reflection. Even though the Israelites were God's chosen people, they were not permitted into the presence of God within the tabernacle but were cut off by a thick veil. God had to keep His presence veiled from the people, because they could not look on His glory and survive.

However, when Jesus came to this earth and died on the cross, the veil in the temple was torn asunder (see Matthew 27:51). It was ripped from the top to the bottom, which suggests that God Himself eagerly tore the veil away from His presence. God was making it clear to His people that He would no longer remove Himself from them, and that His children would henceforth have free access into His presence.

The writer of Hebrews wrote, "Therefore, brethren, having boldness to enter the Holiest by the blood of Jesus, by a new and living way which He consecrated for us, through the veil, that is, His flesh, and having a High Priest over the house of God, let us draw near with a true heart in full assurance of faith, having our hearts sprinkled from an evil conscience and our bodies washed with pure water" (Hebrews 10:19–22).

We reflect God's glory to the world around us—if we first draw close to Him. Moses spent time on Mount Sinai in communion with the Lord, and when he returned to the camp his face was glowing brilliantly with a reflection of God's glory. He was unaware of it, but the people were so startled that they were afraid to come near him. God's glory rested on him to such a degree that his presence was nearly as frightening to them as the presence of God Himself—so much so that he had to cover his face with a veil.

That glow faded, however, as Moses spent time away from God's presence. It was only when he was again in God's presence that the glory to his countenance "recharged," for it was actually a reflection of God's glory rather than some holiness or power within himself. In the same way, as Christians we reflect the character of God as we spend time in His presence. The people with whom we interact on a daily basis can see the character of God reflected in our lives through our actions and attitudes, even when we are sometimes unaware of it ourselves.

However, that outward "glow" can fade when we fail to spend time in His presence. It is important, therefore, for us to spend time with God on a regular basis. Personal Bible reading and prayer, collective worship, and sound biblical teaching are all ways that we deepen our fellowship with God and our fervor for His glory. As Jesus said, "You are the light of the world. A city that is set on a hill cannot be hidden. Nor do they light a lamp and put it under a basket, but on a lampstand, and it gives light to all who are in the house. Let your light so shine before men, that they may see your good works and glorify your Father in heaven" (Matthew 5:14–16).

REFLECTING ON THE TEXT

5) How did Moses demonstrate the qualities of godly leadership? How can you imitate him in your own areas of leadership?

_____

_____

_____

6) Why did Moses ask to see God's glory? If you had been in his place, what would you have asked?

_____

_____

_____

7) Why is it that no man can see the face of God and live? What does this reveal about God's glory? About man's sinful condition?

_____

_____

_____

8) How do you draw into God's presence? What can you do to deepen your understanding of His character?

_____

_____

_____

PERSONAL RESPONSE

9) Are you a friend of God? What can you do to deepen that friendship?

_____

_____

_____

10) How much of God's glory do people see in your life? What might be
veiling that glory from their view?

_____

_____

_____

7

Building the Tabernacle

Exodus 35:1–36:38; 39:32–40:43

Drawing Near

The Israelites were required to follow strict guidelines in constructing the tabernacle and the items that went into it. How would you gauge your ability in following detailed instructions? What challenges would you have faced if you were one of the artisans?

_____

_____

_____

The Context

As we have seen, when the Lord gathered the Israelites near Mount Sinai, He gave them specific instructions on how they were to live and worship Him. These instructions included detailed plans on building a portable tabernacle they would use for worship during their travels in the wilderness. The tabernacle consisted of an open courtyard, surrounded by curtains, that the people of Israel were permitted to enter. Within that courtyard was a smaller tent divided into two parts. The outer portion was the Holy Place, and only the priests were permitted to enter it.

Within the Holy Place was the Most Holy Place, where the Ark of the Covenant was kept. This gorgeous and ornate box with golden cherubim carved on top was constructed according to a specific blueprint from God (see Exodus 25:10–22). The Most Holy Place was the area in which the Lord symbolically resided among His people, and only the high priest was permitted to enter this area one time each year. Anyone other than the high priest who entered the Most Holy Place was struck dead.

The tabernacle contained many elements that required a great wealth of raw materials and skilled craftsmen to create. Although the Israelites had lived for many generations as slaves making bricks, it is possible that some of them had been employed as craftsmen and artisans in Egypt. Whatever the people's level of training, God would now specially enable certain individuals to build the tabernacle to His specific standards, such that the end product would be of exceeding quality and beauty. The fact the people were able to construct something so exquisite while living in the wilderness bears testimony to the supernatural enablement they received from God.

The lesson we will learn in these passages is that the Lord never commands us to do something without giving us the things we need. He provided the Israelites with a great wealth of materials when they left Egypt, and He endowed certain people with the skills that were needed for the construction. One of the greatest gifts of all is given freely to all Christians: the presence of God's Holy Spirit in their lives, who enables them to do *whatever* God calls them to do.

Keys to the Text

Read Exodus 35:1–36:38, noting the key words and phrases indicated below.

A TEAM EFFORT: The work of creating the tabernacle will require the efforts of many people in the camp. In fact, it will involve the entire nation of Israel.

5. TAKE FROM AMONG YOU AN OFFERING: The people were given the opportunity to freely contribute to the nation's worship center by contributing materials needed to build the tabernacle. One wonders how much of their contribution came from Egyptian homes and had been given to them right before the exodus (see Exodus 12:35–36).

11. THE TABERNACLE: Five different names are given for the tabernacle: (1) "sanctuary," denoting a sacred place; (2) "tent," denoting a temporary or collapsible dwelling; (3) "tabernacle," from "to dwell," denoting the place of God's presence; (4) "tabernacle of the congregation, or meeting"; and (5) "tabernacle of the testimony."

13. SHOWBREAD: Each week a new batch of twelve loaves of bread was laid on a table on the north side of the Holy Place. Unlike food placed in pagan shrines and temples, the showbread was not set out to feed Israel's God but to acknowledge that the twelve tribes were sustained constantly under the watchful eye and care of their Lord.

14. THE LAMPSTAND: Situated opposite the table of showbread stood an ornate lampstand, or menorah, patterned after a flowering almond tree. It provided light for the priests serving in the Holy Place. Care was taken, according to God's instructions, to keep it well supplied with pure olive oil so that it would not be extinguished.

CALLED BY GOD: God now calls two specific individuals—Bezalel and Aholiab—to design artistic works for the tabernacle.

31. FILLED HIM WITH THE SPIRIT OF GOD: Only certain individuals in the Old Testament are described as "filled with the Spirit of God," as it was a unique anointing prior to Christ. But Jesus sent God's Holy Spirit to His people, and the Spirit now indwells all Christians. Furthermore, the Holy Spirit provides each believer with spiritual gifts that are to be used in the service of God.

34. THE ABILITY TO TEACH: The Lord also gave Bezalel and Aholiab skill in teaching their trades. This indicates that they were most probably the supervisors or leaders of the construction teams.

36:1. EVERY GIFTED ARTISAN: The Lord had evidently also sent His Spirit on others in Israel at this time, equipping them also to do the skilled work required for the tabernacle. God, as He does even today, had gifted and equipped each individual for the task He had required of them.

FREELY GIVING: The people of Israel join together to create God's tabernacle, using their gifts and possessions generously—even to the point of excess.

2. EVERYONE WHOSE HEART WAS STIRRED: The Lord did not force His people into conscripted service, for to do so would have merely turned Israel

from one slavery to another. Instead He called the Israelites to serve Him willingly, with a glad heart.

3. THE OFFERING WHICH THE CHILDREN OF ISRAEL HAD BROUGHT: All the people of Israel, not just Bezalel and Aholiab, participated in the construction of the tabernacle. There were other craftsmen who worked under the guidance of these two men, others who served the workmen in behind-the-scenes ministries, and the entire nation of Israel contributed the materials that were needed. Today, as then, God calls all His children to be actively involved in His great work, and no job is more necessary than another for the final completion of the task. In the case of the tabernacle, if any function had not been done, the work itself would not have been finished.

FREEWILL OFFERINGS: Note there was no compulsion for God's people to provide the materials for the tabernacle—the Lord relied entirely on His people's generosity. Using our gifts for God's service and sharing from our material blessings should be a joy, not a grudging chore.

5. THE PEOPLE BRING MUCH MORE THAN ENOUGH: This was one of Israel's happier times, when the people poured out to God their gratitude for His countless blessings. This should be our response as well: giving generously and freely to God's work and to His people simply because we are grateful for all that He has given us.

6. THE PEOPLE WERE RESTRAINED FROM BRINGING: Literally, the people were "held back" from bringing any more gifts. The implication is that they had to be almost physically restrained, as their zeal and generosity was so great.

BUILDING THE TABERNACLE: *The Lord gives Moses specific instructions on how to build the tabernacle, and the artisans follow these instructions to the letter.*

8. TEN CURTAINS: The beauty of these curtains could be seen only from the inside, as the thick outer covering of goats' hair drapes and ram and badger skins hid them from the view of anyone except the priests who entered.

FINE LINEN: Egypt had a reputation for producing finely twined linens.

BLUE, PURPLE, AND SCARLET THREAD: These colors were produced by dying the thread: blue from a shellfish, purple from the secretion of a murex snail, and crimson from powdered eggs and bodies of certain worms that attached themselves to holly plants. Deriving different colored dyes from different natural sources demonstrates a substantial degree of technical sophistication with textiles and fabrics.

CHERUBIM: Cherubim, associated with the majestic glory and presence of God, were appropriately woven into the tabernacle curtains and the veil for the Holy of Holies, for this place was where God was present with His people.

13. CLASPS OF GOLD: The technology of the day was sufficient to refine gold.

14. ELEVEN CURTAINS: The extra length of the outer drapes doubled as a covering for the front and back of the tabernacle structure.

19. RAM SKINS DYED RED: With all the wool removed and then dyed, it resembled Moroccan leather.

20. ACACIA WOOD: A hard, durable, close-grained, and aromatic desert wood avoided by wood-eating insects. It was considered good for cabinet making and could also be found in sufficient quantities in the Sinai peninsula.

Read Exodus 39:32–40:38, noting the key words and phrases indicated below.

FINAL REVIEW: The work on the tabernacle is completed, and the people bring each of the items to be used in its operation to Moses for one last review.

32. THUS ALL THE WORK . . . WAS FINISHED: Finally, the moment had arrived when all the different tasks were completed and the result was ready for formal presentation to Israel's leader. No individual artisan was singled out for special mention or award; instead, the whole nation was represented as doing everything in accordance with the Lord's instructions to Moses.

33. THEY BROUGHT THE TABERNACLE TO MOSES: None of the individual parts in the list that follows, nor the sum of them, reflect mere human ingenuity in designing something the people wanted to have but what their Lord required them to have. It was fully His architecture and His design at every level of the undertaking.

35. THE ARK OF THE TESTIMONY: The ark was the most sacred of the furniture in the tabernacle. It housed a copy of the Ten Commandments, which summarized the whole covenant. In Scripture, the ark is also called "the ark of the covenant" (Joshua 3:11) and "the holy ark" (2 Chronicles 35:3).

MERCY SEAT: The lid or cover of the ark was the mercy seat or the place at which atonement took place.

36. THE TABLE: The table of showbread was a stand on which the offerings were placed. The twelve loaves of bread representing the twelve tribes of Israel were always in God's presence.

ALL ITS UTENSILS: Not only was the table for the showbread made of gold, but the utensils for the table were also made of gold.

37. THE LAMPS SET IN ORDER: The gold lampstand held seven lamps, or shallow bowls, in which a wick lay with one end in the oil of the bowl and the lighted end hanging out.

38. GOLD ALTAR: This altar located inside the tabernacle was much smaller than the altar of burnt offering located outside. The incense burned on the altar was a perfume of sweet-smelling aroma.

39. BRONZE ALTAR: This piece of equipment, situated in the courtyard of the tabernacle, was used for animal sacrifices. It was covered not in gold as the items inside the Holy Place, but in bronze. Like the other pieces of furniture and equipment, it was also built to be carried by poles.

LAVER WITH ITS BASE: The priests would come to this large basin for cleansing. The washing of hands and feet was mandatory before engaging in priestly duties.

43. MOSES LOOKED OVER ALL THE WORK: Moses, the one who had been with God on the mount and had passed on the blueprints for everything connected with the tabernacle, now personally inspected the work and confirmed its successful completion. The term *work* is to be taken as "the end result of professional and skilled craftsmen."

MOSES BLESSED THEM: By this act, Moses set his final and formal seal of approval on the outcome and expressed his prayer-wish that good would result to them from their God. This is the only instance recorded in Exodus of Moses' pronouncing a blessing on his people.

THE ARRIVAL: *The time has come for the tabernacle to be erected from all the parts the artisans created. When it is complete, the glory of the Lord comes down and descends over it.*

40:2: YOU SHALL SET UP THE TABERNACLE: The time arrived for the tabernacle to be erected, with the Holy of Holies and its accompanying Holy

Place to the west, and the courtyard entrance to the east. In terms of pagan religions and their worship of the sun god, some polemic significance might be seen in the high priest worshiping God with his back to the rising sun. All who entered the courtyard also turned their backs to the rising sun as they came in to sacrifice and worship.

12. WASH THEM WITH WATER: Washing or bathing was used in both religious and cultural settings. In a religious setting, washing with water symbolized spiritual cleansing, the preparation necessary for entering God's presence. This ritual washing was an important step in the purification of the priests for service in the tabernacle. In a cultural setting, the custom of washing a guest's feet was an important part of hospitality. It was still practiced in New Testament times (see Genesis 18:4; John 13:5).

17. THE TABERNACLE WAS RAISED UP: The tabernacle was completed almost one year after the people's exodus from Egypt. The people were at the foot of Mount Sinai at that time, where the book of Leviticus was given in the first month of that second year. The record of Numbers begins with the people still at Mount Sinai in the second month of that second year after leaving Egypt (see Numbers 1:1).

34. THE CLOUD COVERED . . . THE GLORY OF THE LORD FILLED: This was the final confirmation for Moses and the people that all the work for setting up God's dwelling place had been properly done and all the detailed instructions obediently followed.

36. CLOUD WAS TAKEN UP: This first occurred fifty days after the tabernacle was finished and erected.

UNLEASHING THE TEXT

1) What roles did various people play in constructing the tabernacle? Who was included in the work?

_____

_____

_____

_____

2) If you had been present during this time, what role might you have
   played in the construction?

_____

_____

_____

3) Why did God give Bezalel and Aholiab the ability to teach others?
   What principle does this passage teach us about how God equips
   people to accomplish His work?

_____

_____

_____

4) Why were the people so eager to give their material possessions for the
   tabernacle? What did this reveal about the character of God?

_____

_____

_____

EXPLORING THE MEANING

The Lord gives us what we need for His service. The Lord had commanded the
nation of Israel to create a portable tabernacle to use in worship during their
travels in the wilderness. He gave Moses strict instructions on what to create,
how to create it, and what it would look like when finished. Many of these
articles, such as the ark of the covenant, were intricate and ornate. They were
beautiful works of art that required skills in areas such as metal smithing, gem
cutting, and textile weaving.

The Israelites, however, had been slaves for many generations, and most of them had few skills beyond making bricks. Furthermore, they were living in the desert. They carried all their possessions in a huge caravan, and they did not have access to raw materials. But the Lord did not command His people to do things they could not accomplish. He gave a special endowment of gifts to specific individuals to perform the artistry, and He had already given the people of Israel great riches from the Egyptians that could be used for the raw materials.

This same principle applies to the Lord's people today. He gives us natural talents that can be used for His glory, and He provides spiritual gifts that are specifically designed to meet some need in the people around us. He even gives us the work that earns our income. Most of all, He gives us His Holy Spirit, who teaches us how to become more like Christ.

Our gifts should be used for God's glory. God gave Bezalel and Aholiab special gifts that enabled them to be master craftsmen in a wide variety of trades—from working with metals to shaping precious stones to building ornate furniture and weaving gorgeous textiles. These gifts could have made them wealthy, had they chosen to use those skills to create beautiful objects that they could then sell for profit. But that is not what these men did.

Bezalel and Aholiab understood the Lord had given them a special anointing for the specific purpose of creating His tabernacle. The finished tabernacle would be for God's glory, not their own. In the same way, the gifts that God gives to us—whether spiritual or material—are to be used for His glory, not for our own.

This does not mean it is wrong for us to earn a living using the gifts and talents that the Lord has given. In fact, all good things come from His hand. But the Lord gives us gifts so that we can share them with others, not use them for our own gratification. "Even so you, since you are zealous for spiritual gifts, let it be for the edification of the church that you seek to excel" (1 Corinthians 14:12).

The Lord loves a cheerful giver. It is moving to picture the people of Israel being so eager to participate in building the Lord's tabernacle that they poured out their material goods like water. Every morning they came burdened with gold and silver and cloth and precious gems to be used as raw materials by the craftsmen.

It is true, of course, that they owned these possessions because God had given them favor in the eyes of the Egyptians and they had been given the goods freely as they departed. However, this fact may have been the very motivation behind the people's generosity: they recognized they would not even own such precious possessions if the Lord had not provided them in the first place. The Israelites gave generously and freely, not under any compulsion, and they gave to the point that they had to be restrained from giving further.

This should be our attitude as well. We should always remember that our material possessions are all provided by the Lord—even the very income that we work for—and He wants us to share freely with others. "So let each one give as he purposes in his heart, not grudgingly or of necessity; for God loves a cheerful giver. And God is able to make all grace abound toward you, that you, always having all sufficiency in all things, may have an abundance for every good work" (2 Corinthians 9:7–8).

REFLECTING ON THE TEXT

5) Read Ephesians 5:18–21. What does it mean to be "filled with the Spirit" of God? What effect does such a filling have on a person's life? What are some of the results of a Spirit-filled life?

_____

_____

_____

6) What role does wisdom play in us using our spiritual and material gifts? What might be an unwise use of those gifts?

_____

_____

_____

_____

7) In what ways were all the roles of building the tabernacle equally necessary? Why do people sometimes think that some roles in spiritual service are more important than others?

_____

_____

_____

8) Why was it essential for the people to carry out the work to the letter of God's specification? Why was their obedience in this instance so important to God?

_____

_____

_____

PERSONAL RESPONSE

9) What gifts—spiritual, innate, or material—has the Lord given you? How are you using them to bring glory to God?

_____

_____

_____

10) Do you give to the Lord's work cheerfully or grudgingly? What motivates you to give?

_____

_____

_____

8

COMPLAINTS AND REBELLION
Numbers 11:1–12:16

DRAWING NEAR

What guidelines do you set when it comes to evaluating a leader? How would you describe the difference between constructive criticism and complaining?

_____

_____

_____

THE CONTEXT

The Israelites had been traveling through the wilderness for about a year. During that time, they had again and again witnessed the Lord's immense power and miraculous intervention. One miracle in particular had taken place twice a day for that entire time. Each morning and evening, the Lord rained down a unique wafer-like substance called *manna*—a nutritious and tasty food direct from the Lord Himself.

This wonder was profound. The food was so nourishing that the people did not need to eat anything else. They never got hungry, it tasted good—like wafers made with honey—and they did not need to go out and hunt for it or gather it from bushes. All the people had to do was merely step outside their tents and pick it up off the ground. The Lord delivered it right to their doorsteps!

Best of all, there was always more than enough manna for everyone, so no one ever went hungry or unsatisfied. What was left over would melt away in the morning sun, with the exception of the manna collected on the day before the Sabbath. That manna would miraculously *not* disappear, and it would sustain the people on their day of rest. There was so much of God's love in the manna that it is hard to believe anyone would have complained about it.

But that is just what the people did. A few started grumbling about their meatless diet, remembering the varied foods they had enjoyed in Egypt, while conveniently forgetting the dreadful slave labor by which they had earned it. The murmuring soon spread from a few to many, and before long the entire nation of Israel was rebelling against the Lord—just because He hadn't rained down some meat along with the manna! As inconceivable as this may sound, it is no different from rebellion among God's people today, a sin that God detests as much as witchcraft.

Keys to the Text

Read Numbers 11:1–12:16, noting the key words and phrases indicated below.

> THE PEOPLE COMPLAIN: *God has been miraculously providing food for the Israelites throughout their sojourn in the wilderness. But they begin to grow dissatisfied.*

1. WHEN THE PEOPLE COMPLAINED: Although the Israelites had been away from Egypt for about a year, their complaining had begun soon after leaving Egypt, when they saw Pharaoh's army coming up behind them. It continued for the next forty years.

FOR THE LORD HEARD IT: We must remember that the Lord hears the words of our mouths and has promised to hold us accountable for what we speak.

HIS ANGER WAS AROUSED: The people's faithless response was inexcusable. Although they had repeatedly seen the Lord's miraculous work, they responded to their current circumstances by grumbling rather than by trusting God. They imputed false motives to God, chose to overlook His past victories, and focused instead on what He had apparently failed to do (based on what *they* wanted Him to do).

2. THE FIRE WAS QUENCHED: God sometimes sent strong discipline on His people when they grumbled. Ingratitude and complaining are sins that we should take seriously (since God certainly does).

3. TABERAH: Meaning "burning."

4. THE MIXED MULTITUDE: There were Egyptians and others who left Egypt with the people of Israel.

LUSTING FOR MEAT: The manna the Lord provides to the Israelites is more than enough to sustain them while they are in the wilderness. But they desire for something more.

INTENSE CRAVING: The Hebrew phrase is literally "desire desire." The people were lusting for meat.

WHO WILL GIVE US MEAT: This is an indirect insult to the Lord, for the answer to the question is "God will!" He had provided them with water, food, shade from the sun, light in the darkness, and every other physical need. In the face of this accusatory question, the Lord must have felt as insulted as he did over King David's lust: "And if that had been too little, I also would have given you much more!" (2 Samuel 12:8).

5. WE REMEMBER THE FISH WHICH WE ATE FREELY IN EGYPT: But the people had evidently forgotten the horrible cost they had paid to get those foods. The Lord had made it clear to Israel that if they obeyed Him, they would only be in the wilderness a relatively short time. They were briefly "making do" without meat until they arrived at the land that would flow with milk and honey.

6. NOTHING AT ALL EXCEPT THIS MANNA BEFORE OUR EYES: Notice the wording of this complaint: "nothing at all except *this manna*." This expressed contempt for God's good gift and suggested the people were literally getting fed up with it. Grumbling is a form of rebellion against God, and it grows out of ingratitude.

8. GROUND IT ON MILLSTONES OR BEAT IT IN THE MORTAR: Manna evidently served equally well as flour and could be used in a wide variety of dishes. Of course, there was not an abundance of other ingredients available, but again,

that situation was only intended to be temporary. Soldiers, sailors, explorers, and others have subsisted for much longer on much less than the Israelites possessed.

Moses Is Fed Up: The people are hungry for meat, but Moses is completely fed up with their constant complaining. The Lord, too, is displeased.

10. MOSES ALSO WAS DISPLEASED: The complaints about the manna were casting aspersions on Moses' leadership, and he was becoming discouraged.

11. WHY HAVE YOU AFFLICTED YOUR SERVANT: Moses was so moved by the people's ingratitude that he, in turn, poured out a lament before the Lord. His feelings were understandable, yet he too was accusing the Lord of false motives. God had not "afflicted" Moses with leadership—his role brought with it great blessings and privileges, not the least of which was speaking face-to-face with the Lord as a man speaks to a friend. This alone was enough to prove that Moses had found favor with the Lord, yet at this moment he was accusing Him of the opposite.

13. THEY WEEP ALL OVER ME: This is a wonderful depiction of the Israelites' whining. They were crying like spoiled children, throwing a tantrum because they couldn't have what they wanted for supper.

14. I AM NOT ABLE TO BEAR ALL THESE PEOPLE ALONE: This was actually quite true, but Moses was losing sight of the fact that he did *not* bear the burden alone—the Lord bore it for him. This is the mark of a person who is trying to accomplish the Lord's work in his own strength. When we do this, discouragement and weariness quickly set in.

15. PLEASE KILL ME HERE AND NOW: Elijah prayed a similar prayer when he felt alone: "It is enough! Now, LORD, take my life, for I am no better than my fathers! . . . I have been very zealous for the LORD God of hosts; for the children of Israel have forsaken Your covenant, torn down Your altars, and killed Your prophets with the sword. I alone am left; and they seek to take my life" (1 Kings 19:4, 9–10). We are indeed fortunate that the lord does not grant everything we request.

17. THAT YOU MAY NOT BEAR IT YOURSELF ALONE: The Lord showed His mercy toward Moses by giving him seventy men to assist him in the work of leading the people. The Israelites were a vast multitude, more than 600,000 strong, and the duties of leadership must have been a constant burden.

SATISFYING THEIR LUSTS: The Lord grants the people's request for meat—to the uttermost. He allows them to satisfy their lust and discover that lust is never truly satisfied.

18. YOU SHALL EAT MEAT: There are times when the Lord will give us *exactly* what we ask for, but at the same time He will send leanness into our souls (see Psalm 106:13–15).

20. UNTIL IT COMES OUT OF YOUR NOSTRILS: The people's lust for meat was so unbridled that the Lord determined to satisfy it to the extent that it would become loathsome to them. This is a common consequence that comes from gratifying the lusts of the flesh. Lusts of any description, when gratified, soon cease to be pleasurable and become merely a disgusting addiction.

YOU HAVE DESPISED THE LORD: At the foundation of complaining is a hatred for the Lord. The people were effectively saying they hated God and His provisions and would have preferred to remain slaves to the Egyptians.

23. HAS THE LORD'S ARM BEEN SHORTENED: The Lord's patience and mercy toward His people were truly remarkable. Again and again He provided for them, and again and again they rebelled against Him. In spite of this, the Lord continued to patiently demonstrate that He had been faithful in the past and would be in the future.

SEVENTY PROPHETS: In response to Moses' complaints, God commands him to appoint seventy elders to assist him in his leadership duties. These men are suddenly filled with God's Spirit.

24. HE GATHERED THE SEVENTY MEN OF THE ELDERS: In response to Moses' despair in leading the people, the Lord gave him seventy men to help. (These aides might be the same seventy referred to in Exodus 18:21–26.)

25. TOOK OF THE SPIRIT . . . AND PLACED THE SAME UPON THE SEVENTY: This refers to the Spirit of God. It was by means of the Holy Spirit that Moses was able to lead Israel, and there the Lord gave that Spirit to the seventy elders.

THEY PROPHESIED: Here, the prophesying refers to the giving of praise and similar expressions of worship to the Lord without prior training. The text is clear this was a one-time event as far as these men were concerned.

29. OH, THAT ALL THE LORD'S PEOPLE WERE PROPHETS: Moses demonstrated once again the meekness of his character. Instead of being

threatened by the prophesying of these elders, he rejoiced that the Lord had poured out His Spirit on them. His desire looked forward to the day when all of God's people would have His Spirit within them. Despite all this, however, the people would soon rise up against Moses and accuse him of lording it over them.

HERE COMES THE QUAIL: As promised, the Lord sends meat to the people in the form of a flock of quail. But the people's lust for meat will come at a terrible price.

31. FLUTTERING NEAR THE CAMP: The Lord, using a wind, brought a great quantity of quail that surrounded the encampment within one day's journey. The birds flew at a height of about three feet ("two cubits") where they were able to be easily captured or clubbed to the ground by the people.

32. THE PEOPLE STAYED UP ALL THAT DAY, ALL NIGHT, AND ALL THE NEXT DAY: The people went into a frenzy as they ran about clubbing birds to satisfy their appetites. It was a frightening picture.

TEN HOMERS: Approximately sixty to seventy bushels—and that was the *least* that anyone gathered. The Lord was more than providing—He was sending a surfeit.

33. WHILE THE MEAT WAS STILL BETWEEN THEIR TEETH: This is a graphic depiction of the people gratifying their physical lust. There is no suggestion the meat even tasted good to the people or was in any way satisfying; it was merely being chewed and swallowed in a gluttonous food fest.

34. KIBROTH HATTAAVAH: Literally "graves of craving." God sent a severe plague in response to the people's lust, and as a result many died on account of their rebellious ingratitude and sinful cravings. "Each one is tempted when he is drawn away by his own desires and enticed. Then, when desire has conceived, it gives birth to sin; and sin, when it is full-grown, brings forth death" (James 1:14–15).

MIRIAM AND AARON REBEL: The prophesying of the seventy elders apparently leads Miriam and Aaron to be jealous of Moses' authority. Their dissatisfaction is a precursor to rebellion.

12:1. MIRIAM AND AARON: This revolt must have been especially painful for Moses, as his own brother and sister were betraying him.

THE ETHIOPIAN WOMAN WHOM HE HAD MARRIED: Although the term *Ethiopian* could refer to Zipporah, Moses' first wife, it seems more likely that Moses had recently remarried after Zipporah's death. Miriam and Aaron were likely using this marriage as an excuse for rebelling against Moses, though the real issue was Moses' role as the Lord's spokesman. Miriam was mentioned first, so she was probably the instigator of the attack against Moses.

2. HAS THE LORD INDEED SPOKEN ONLY THROUGH MOSES: The true motivation for Miriam and Aaron's rebellion appears to be linked to the seventy men prophesying. Rather than rejoicing that the Lord had extended His Spirit to others, as Moses had done, Miriam and Aaron began to view their brother's Spirit-filled leadership with contempt. Miriam and Aaron apparently wanted to be included, claiming that God had spoken to them in the same way He had spoken to Moses.

4. SUDDENLY: The Lord's wrath fell on the people suddenly and without warning. This is a terrifying situation, yet the New Testament warns us that the Lord's wrath will finally fall upon the earth just as suddenly (see 2 Peter 3:10).

8. I SPEAK WITH HIM FACE TO FACE: Moses was not just a spokesman for the Lord but also the Lord's *friend*. The Lord did not speak to Moses through visions and dreams, but plainly and directly. In this, Moses was incredibly privileged.

WHY THEN WERE YOU NOT AFRAID: It is a serious matter to rebel against the Lord's leaders—both inside and outside of the church (see Hebrews 13:17). The Scriptures make it clear that Christians are to submit themselves to people in authority, even in a secular and ungodly society (see 1 Peter 2:13–15).

MIRIAM BECOMES A LEPER: The Lord strikes Miriam immediately with leprosy, and she is removed from the camp. But He also shows His mercy and grace.

10. SUDDENLY MIRIAM BECAME LEPROUS: Miriam had sinned openly, and the results of that rebellion would be equally public. Lepers were utterly shunned by the people and were forced to live outside the camp in a place of dishonor. Leprosy, like the sin of grumbling, was contagious.

11. IN WHICH WE HAVE SINNED: God's people must understand the gravity of rebellion. To speak evil against the leaders God has appointed is a grievous sin.

14. **If her father had but spit in her face:** If a father spat in the face of his daughter, it would indicate that she had somehow disgraced the family name. The Lord was saying that Miriam's rebellious spirit was a disgrace to the name of God. Grumbling and rebellion discredit God's name before the world around us, because such actions demonstrate emphatically that God's own people do not respect Him.

Afterward she may be received again: Nevertheless, the Lord once again displayed His grace. He did not strike Miriam dead, as He would have been justified in doing, nor did He leave her a leper. He instructed her to be segregated from the rest of the people for seven days, after which she would be fully restored into the camp.

Unleashing the Text

1) If you had been traveling in the desert for a year, eating manna twice a day, what would your attitude be toward your diet?

_____

_____

_____

_____

2) What led the people of Israel to complain about the lack of meat? What does this reveal about complaining?

_____

_____

_____

_____

3) Why did the Lord give the people meat "until it came out of their nostrils"? What does this reveal about lust?

_____

_____

_____

4) What led Miriam and Aaron to rebel against Moses? How did their attitude differ from Moses' attitude?

_____

_____

_____

EXPLORING THE MEANING

Choose to be content where the Lord has placed you. The Lord had led His people into a desert region devoid of food and water to demonstrate how He would provide for all their needs. He rained manna on them twice a day and provided water miraculously, but the people grew tired of these provisions. They complained about eating "nothing at all except this manna before our eyes" (Numbers 11:6) and grumbled about not having any meat in their diet.

This demonstrates an important principle of happiness: we *choose* whether or not we will be content. Contentment comes when we remember to be grateful for what the Lord has given us. If the Israelites had remembered each day to praise the Lord for His miraculous provision of food and water—focusing on the good things they *did* have—they would not have focused on the meat they *didn't* have. They would have been content, and the Lord would have been glorified.

Paul wrote, "I have learned in whatever state I am, to be content" (Philippians 4:11). This is an excellent pattern for the body of Christ to emulate, because "godliness with contentment is great gain . . . But those who desire to be

93

rich fall into temptation and a snare, and into many foolish and harmful lusts which drown men in destruction and perdition" (1 Timothy 6:6–9).

Lust is never truly satisfied. The Israelites told themselves they could be completely satisfied *if only* they had some meat. This is the nature of lust—it is an "if only" mindset that causes us to focus on the one thing we don't have rather than on the many things we do have. "*If only* I had this, I'd be happy." "*If only* I had that, I'd be fulfilled." Lust is the natural outgrowth of a lack of contentment.

Lust is problematic in that it leads us to disobey God's commands in trying to satisfy our sinful desires. Furthermore, even if we do gain the one thing we felt was missing, it will not bring us lasting happiness. There will only be another missing thing in back of it, another "if only" to replace the present one. Lust compels us to do anything and everything to satisfy that desire, and it inevitably leads us to violate the Lord's commands.

The Israelites indulged their lust for meat, and it led them to rebel against the Lord. Peter warned the New Testament church to refrain from likewise seeking to fulfill the lust of the flesh: "Beloved, I beg you as sojourners and pilgrims, abstain from fleshly lusts which war against the soul" (1 Peter 2:11).

Rebellion is like the sin of witchcraft. In 1 Samuel 15:23, the prophet Samuel told King Saul that "rebellion is as the sin of witchcraft." The Lord's response to rebellion among the Israelites was swift and strong. In this instance Miriam was stricken with leprosy, and on other occasions during the Israelites' journey God's response would be equally as strong. The Lord hates a rebellious spirit, just as He hates witchcraft.

The reason for this is because a rebellious spirit is actually *the same in its essence* as witchcraft and idolatry. When we grumble about the Lord's provision in our lives, we are rebelling against His leadership and authority. When we rebel against the Lord, we are setting ourselves up in His place as lord of our lives. This is the same sin that Satan committed when he declared himself to be equal with God.

God has pronounced woe on all who rebel against Him: "Woe to the rebellious children . . . who take counsel, but not of Me, and who devise plans, but not of My Spirit, that they may add sin to sin" (Isaiah 30:1). Worse, God considers every rebel His *foe*—and actually fights them. "They rebelled and grieved His Holy Spirit; so He turned Himself against them as an enemy, and He fought against them" (Isaiah 63:10).

REFLECTING ON THE TEXT

5) Why were the Israelites not content with manna? What is needed to find contentment?

_____

_____

_____

6) How does lust differ from normal and righteous desires? How did the Israelites' lust for meat differ from physical hunger?

_____

_____

_____

7) In what ways is a complaining spirit the same as a rebellious spirit? How can one person's grumbling lead to open rebellion?

_____

_____

_____

8) Why does God hate rebellion? In what ways is rebellion like the sin of witchcraft?

_____

_____

_____

Personal Response

9) Are you content where the Lord has placed you? If not, what must you change in yourself to find contentment? (Remember, contentment comes from a change of heart, not from a change of circumstances.)

_____

_____

_____

10) Do you have a complaining spirit or a submissive spirit? How do submissiveness and contentment reinforce one another?

_____

_____

_____

9

AT THE DOORSTEP
Numbers 13:16–14:38

DRAWING NEAR

The Israelites often suffered from a lack of proper perspective. In what ways
does a person's perspective define his or her reality?

_____

_____

_____

THE CONTEXT

As we saw in the previous study, the Israelites often brought misfortune on
themselves by choosing to complain and disobey God. Yet in spite of these set-
backs, God led them on until they arrived at the banks of the Jordan River, the
border to the Promised Land. Israel was on the doorstep, and God was about to
fulfill His promise to give them a land flowing with milk and honey. So Moses
sent twelve men, one from each tribe of Israel, to spy out the land and plan a
military strategy.

The spies soon discovered the land was already populated. What's more,
the people who lived there were powerful—and some of them were giants! It's
true the land was fertile—it took two men to carry a bunch of grapes—but

how were the Israelites to defeat such powerful armies? This, at least, was the perspective of ten of the spies. Two of the spies, Joshua and Caleb, saw things differently.

Joshua had been serving as Moses' personal assistant during the trek from Egypt. We know little about Caleb's background, but what we do know is that he had the right attitude toward God. Both he and Joshua agreed that while there were powerful armies and walled cities in Canaan—and even giants— God was more powerful. He would conquer these enemies just as He had conquered Pharaoh's army.

Joshua and Caleb focused on the fact that God's word had been true concerning the richness of the land, so His word would also prove true concerning the enemies who lived there. In this way, they demonstrated they had complete faith in the character of God. They proved to be men of great courage, and we can learn much from their attitude.

KEYS TO THE TEXT

Read Numbers 13:16–14:38, noting the key words and phrases indicated below.

> SPYING OUT THE LAND: *The Israelites arrive at the Jordan River and are poised to take the land that God has promised to them. But first Moses sends twelve men to spy out the region.*

16. THE MEN WHOM MOSES SENT TO SPY OUT THE LAND: The Israelites had been traveling through the wilderness, safe now from any pursuing armies, and had arrived at the Jordan River. As they looked across the river at the Promised Land, they were certain their exodus from Egypt was nearly over. But before they could enter the land of milk and honey, they wanted to see what the enemy within was made of.

HOSHEA THE SON OF NUN: Moses changed his assistant's name from Hoshea, which means "desire for salvation," to Joshua, which means "the Lord is salvation." The difference in meaning is subtle but significant. The young man had originally desired salvation, and now he had found it in the Lord Himself. The fact that Moses changed his name indicates that Joshua was already under his close supervision.

17. SPY OUT THE LAND OF CANAAN: Moses never doubted the Lord would provide victory for His people as they entered Canaan. His intention in sending out these spies was to plan strategy, not to determine whether or not they could defeat their enemies. The Lord wants His people to trust Him in all things, but we are also called to live responsibly—including planning ahead as much as is humanly possible.

20. BE OF GOOD COURAGE: This is actually a command, not a mere formulaic statement such as "have a nice day." Moses was commanding the spies to be courageous, warning them in advance not to become overwhelmed with the obstacles that stood between them and their possession of Canaan. Courage is a deliberate choice not to allow fear to take command. Most of the spies, however, would fail in this matter.

THE SEASON OF THE FIRST RIPE GRAPES: That is, mid-July.

21. WILDERNESS OF ZIN: Rehob was northwest of the Sea of Galilee. The spies covered the entire area of the Promised Land.

WHAT THEY FOUND THERE: The spies spend forty days traveling throughout the land of Canaan and return with reports and grapes. Big grapes!

22. HEBRON: This city was of importance to the Israelites because Abraham had built an altar there and because both he and Isaac were buried there. The city had since been fortified by Canaanites. (See the map in the Introduction.)

THE DESCENDANTS OF ANAK: The descendants of Anak were renowned for their great stature, much as Goliath would one day become famous for his size among the Philistines. Ahiman, Sheshai, and Talmai were probably specific men living in Hebron at the time. They may have been famous warriors themselves.

23. THEY CARRIED IT BETWEEN TWO OF THEM ON A POLE: This demonstrates the enormous size and weight of the grapes, as it required two men to carry one bunch. Here was tangible proof of the Lord's promise that Canaan would be abundantly prosperous and nourishing for the people.

26. SHOWED THEM THE FRUIT: The spies were accountable before the Lord for the report they brought back, because their encouragement or

discouragement would influence the nation as a whole. Nevertheless, all the people could see for themselves that the Lord's words were true: the land was indeed flowing with milk and honey.

27. IT TRULY FLOWS WITH MILK AND HONEY: Thus far, the report of the spies was true—at least factually accurate. But what mattered more was their faith that God would conquer the land on their behalf. Had they rejoiced in the fruit rather than lamenting over the giants, their report might have been different.

AND NOW FOR THE BAD NEWS: *The spies have presented all the good news about the land of Canaan. Now they focus on the bad news—and end up departing from fact.*

28. NEVERTHELESS: Here is the actual spirit of the spies' report. After acknowledging the Promised Land did indeed flow with milk and honey, they chose to become obsessed with the obstacles standing in their way from possessing that land.

29. AMALEKITES . . . HITTITES . . . JEBUSITES: The Lord had already told Moses there were people living in the land of Canaan (see Exodus 3:8). Furthermore, He had promised that He would drive out these nations before the Israelites and give them victory after victory. But the people chose to act as though the Lord had not warned them of these inhabitants—almost as if God Himself had been caught by surprise or had deliberately sent them to be slaughtered.

30. CALEB QUIETED THE PEOPLE: Caleb demonstrated his leadership abilities by taking charge when the entire nation of Israel began to rise up against Moses.

WE ARE WELL ABLE TO OVERCOME IT: Caleb also demonstrated that he had complete faith in God's promises. He did not pretend there were no problems to overcome but chose to focus on ways to overcome those obstacles (by focusing on God).

31. THEY ARE STRONGER THAN WE: This was probably true, in military terms, but Pharaoh's elite army had been far stronger than the Israelites as well. Indeed, Egypt was stronger than any army in the Promised Land—and the Lord had utterly destroyed them. The ten spies were placing their faith in their power, not in the power of God.

32. A BAD REPORT: In this, the ten spies sinned greatly. Their report stirred up fear in the people and revealed that the spies themselves did not believe God could be trusted. Their report led the entire nation to lose faith in God and to despair.

A LAND THAT DEVOURS ITS INHABITANTS: This was simply not true. At this point, the spies were bringing a blatantly false report that contradicted the concrete evidence they had brought back.

ALL THE PEOPLE WHOM WE SAW: This, too, was false. There were indeed some giants in the land, but they were probably the exception rather than the rule. When we focus on the problems that confront us rather than on God's power and faithfulness, we begin to exaggerate the situation and are soon overcome with doubt and anxiety.

33. AND SO WE WERE IN THEIR SIGHT: This is another side effect of losing our focus: we begin to worry too much about what other people think and too little about what God thinks. The Canaanites might have considered the Israelites of no consequence, but God thought otherwise. They may also have thought they could defeat and subjugate Israel, but God knew they could not overcome His power. The fact is that the people of Canaan probably did *not* think these things in the first place, for the fear of God had swept over the nations in that area as God led the Israelites from victory to victory.

THE ISRAELITES DESPAIR: The bad report of the spies leads the entire nation of Israel to lose sight of God's faithfulness. Despair and fear set in.

14:1. ALL THE CONGREGATION: Here we see the effect of the negative report the ten spies brought back. As those who had been put in a position of influence, their fear and doubt soon infected the entire nation. Their response was indicative of their rebellious hearts, which lacked faith in God's clear promises.

2. IF ONLY WE HAD DIED IN THIS WILDERNESS: Tragically, that is precisely what happened to those people because of this incident.

3. WHY HAS THE LORD BROUGHT US TO THIS LAND TO FALL BY THE SWORD: The people had made this false accusation against God many times before. The Lord had wrought countless miracles, defeated powerful foes,

removed immovable obstacles, provided for all their physical needs, and even given them a worship place that moved with them wherever they went, yet they still accused Him of being treacherous. God's people commit this same sin today when they forget all His blessings and accuse Him of not caring about their circumstances.

JOSHUA AND CALEB: *Two of the spies refuse to succumb to the despair of the other ten. These men are Joshua and Caleb.*

6. TORE THEIR CLOTHES: Of the twelve spies, only Joshua and Caleb urged the people to trust God and move forward. They tore their clothes as an outward sign of their deep grief and frustration.

7. AN EXCEEDINGLY GOOD LAND: Joshua and Caleb focused on the blessings of the land rather than on the obstacles. All twelve men had the same basic facts to work from, but Joshua and Caleb reached a radically different conclusion. In our own lives, there will be times when obedience to God will seem hard, maybe even impossible. In those instances, we must rely on His character and His promises and choose to trust and obey Him even when it is difficult to do.

8. HE WILL BRING US INTO THIS LAND AND GIVE IT TO US: Here is the nub of Joshua and Caleb's thinking. The ten focused on their own strength, while Joshua and Caleb focused on God's strength.

9. DO NOT . . . FEAR THE PEOPLE OF THE LAND: When we focus on our circumstances, we begin to fear what other people can do to us. This is the same as rebelling against God, according to Joshua and Caleb. Fear is the result of taking our eyes away from God's faithfulness, and it leads us to rebel against Him.

THEY ARE OUR BREAD: The ten spies had said they were like grasshoppers in the sight of the Canaanites. Joshua and Caleb retorted by stating emphatically that God's people would devour the giants like pieces of bread.

DO NOT FEAR THEM: Once again we see a commandment concerning fear. We tend to think of fear as an emotion, and as such beyond our conscious control. But God's Word states repeatedly that we must *choose* not to permit fear to rule our thoughts. When fear rises in our hearts, we must conquer it by deliberately choosing to place our faith in Christ.

GOD'S JUDGMENT FALLS: *The Lord responds to the people's rebellion by decreeing the entire generation will not see the Promised Land. Only Joshua and Caleb will be exceptions.*

22. WHO HAVE SEEN MY GLORY AND THE SIGNS WHICH I DID: The Lord laid out the sins of the people: they had repeatedly seen His miracles and faithfulness, yet they had just as repeatedly put Him to the test and refused to heed His voice. The Israelites' ability to see the strength of their foes should have tested—and proven—their faith in God, but instead they chose to put Him to the test. They did not heed His voice by obeying His repeated injunction to "move forward" but balked at His command and chose to move backward to Egypt. It is a grievous sin to rebel against the Lord.

23. THEY CERTAINLY SHALL NOT SEE THE LAND: As a result of the people's rebellion, the adults (aged twenty and older) would not be permitted to enter the Promised Land. Instead, they would wander about the wilderness for the next forty years, until every one of them had died. There would be only two exceptions to this decree.

24. HE HAS A DIFFERENT SPIRIT IN HIM: Caleb (and Joshua) had demonstrated he was obedient to the Spirit of God, while the rest of the people had demonstrated they were constantly submitting to a spirit of fear.

38. JOSHUA ... AND CALEB ... REMAINED ALIVE: As a result of these two men's faithfulness, the Lord exempted them from the tragic judgment that fell on the rest of the nation. They had set an example of what it means to trust God in all circumstances, focusing on His faithfulness rather than on circumstances.

UNLEASHING THE TEXT

1) If you had been one of the spies, how would you have reacted to seeing giants? To strong, walled cities? To huge grapes?

_____

_____

_____

2) Why did the ten spies say they could not defeat their enemies? Why did they not rejoice in the wealth of the land?

_____

_____

_____

3) Why did Joshua and Caleb say that the Israelites could defeat their enemies? How was their focus different from the others'?

_____

_____

_____

4) If you had been in the Israelite camp, which report do you think you would have listened to? Why?

_____

_____

_____

Exploring the Meaning

Our mental focus affects our faith. Twelve men walked throughout the land of Canaan. They all saw the same things: giants, walled cities, immense grapes, and so forth. Ten of those men, however, determined that Israel could never conquer the land, whereas two were convinced that it would be an easy matter to move in and take possession.

The difference lay in what the spies focused on. Ten of them admitted there were lots of big grapes, but their main concern was with the giants and walled cities. They were focused on the problems that lay ahead of them—and their *own* strength to overcome those problems. Joshua and Caleb, on the other hand, were focused not on the immediate obstacles but on the prize that lay beyond those obstacles. They were concentrating solely on God's power and faithfulness in the past, and that is what convinced them that they could devour their enemies like bread.

This kind of faith is not the power of "positive thinking"; it is a conscious decision—often repeated—to place our trust in God's provision rather than in the problems that stand in our way. God's people are frequently faced with seemingly insurmountable obstacles, but the Lord calls us to rely on His strength to overcome them. "He Himself has said, 'I will never leave you nor forsake you.' So we may boldly say: 'The Lord is my helper; I will not fear. What can man do to me?'" (Hebrews 13:5–6).

We must choose to "be of good courage." God's Word frequently commands us to "be of good courage" and "fear not." These are *commands*, not suggestions or mere words of encouragement. While it is true that the emotion of fear will come on us at times, what we do with that fear *is* a matter of will—and of obedience to God's command.

Joshua and Caleb no doubt experienced the same emotion of fear as the ten other spies. However, because of their greater faith in God's provision, they were able to resist and overcome that natural human emotion. The other ten men unfortunately allowed their fears to shape their judgment and led the entire nation astray.

This principle goes hand in hand with the previous one: our mental focus affects our faith. By consciously focusing our minds on the promises and character of God, our faith is strengthened and enlarged. We are better able to resist fear because we remember the many ways that God has been faithful in the past. It becomes easier and easier for us to trust Him, because we know if He was faithful in the past, He will be faithful in the future. It's consistent with His character. That's the mindset we must have. We resist fear simply by *choosing* to trust God instead.

Our lack of faith may lead others into sin. It is quite likely that the ten spies infected each another with their fear and lack of faith all the way back to the camp. They probably reiterated and reinforced to each other all the terrible dangers that lay ahead in Canaan. It should come as no surprise, then, that when they brought their words of discouragement to the people of Israel, the entire nation was likewise infected by their doubt and negativity.

Focusing on circumstances rather than on God—thereby *losing our faith in His promises*—is a sin. That sin is compounded when our lack of faith infects others. The things that we say matter. Our words affect our *own* attitudes, and they also affect the opinions of those around us. If our speech is filled with fear and woe, we will influence others to be filled with fear and woe. But if our speech is filled with an expectation of God's faithfulness, others will be encouraged to trust Him.

Just as we choose how to respond to fear, so we must choose how to respond to trouble. The Lord permitted the Israelites to face hardships and enemies from time to time in order to test their faith—to strengthen it, just as testing strengthens steel. Our faith is strengthened each time we trust God, and we strengthen the faith of others by showing forth our own faith in Him.

REFLECTING ON THE TEXT

5) What role did the ten spies play in the despair of the nation? What role did each individual person play?

_____

_____

_____

_____

6) Why are we commanded to "be of good courage"? How is this done? In practical terms, how can a person overcome fear?

_____

_____

_____

7) What are some of the things God had done previously to prove to the people that He was in control? Why did these not matter to the Israelites in this passage?

_____

_____

_____

8) What are some of the things the Lord has done in your own life to prove that He is in control? How can these past victories encourage you and help you as you face present or future difficulties?

_____

_____

_____

PERSONAL RESPONSE

9) When have you been affected by someone else's attitude toward hardship? When has your attitude affected others?

_____

_____

_____

10) What do you tend to focus on when circumstances go awry? On a practical level, how can you deepen your trust in God's faithfulness?

_____

_____

_____

10

NO WATER IN THE WILDERNESS

Numbers 20:1–29

DRAWING NEAR

It is easy to get caught up in the belief that if something worked well in the past, it will work well again in the future. What is the danger in this type of thinking?

_____

_____

_____

THE CONTEXT

Moses was a humble man, and his life was characterized by faithful obedience to God. He had been miraculously kept alive when Pharaoh ordered the death of all Hebrew male children, and the Lord had worked events so that Pharaoh's own daughter raised him. In that position he had enjoyed the best that Egypt had to offer, with a lifetime of security and influence in front of him, yet he had abandoned everything in order to identify with God's people, who were the lowest of slaves.

Moses obeyed God's call to lead the people out of bondage in spite of the fact that he felt completely inadequate and unprepared. He spent the rest of his life interceding for the Israelites, acting as an intermediary between them and God, and demonstrating in his own life what it meant to obey the Lord. He did this in the face of constant rebellion and complaints from the people, remaining humbly obedient to God even when the Israelites said that he was unworthy to lead them.

However, even a great man such as Moses was capable of failure in his walk with God. On one notable occasion, as we will see during this study, he lost his temper and failed to follow God's exact command when the people needed water. From a human perspective it was a small lapse, easily excused by the pressures he was under. But his disobedience was significant in God's eyes, and it resulted in his not entering the Promised Land.

Nevertheless, Moses is listed in Hebrews 11 as one of the great heroes of our faith, and his life provides us with an excellent example of walking in obedience.

Keys to the Text

Read Numbers 20:1–29, noting the key words and phrases indicated below.

No Water: After the failure at Kadesh, the Israelites are forced to wander in the wilderness for many years. When they again find themselves without water, they once more begin to grumble and complain.

1. THE CHILDREN OF ISRAEL: This chapter records the beginning of the transition from the old generation, represented by Miriam and Aaron, to the new generation, represented by Eleazar. Geographically, Israel would move from Kadesh to the plains of Moab, where the conquest of the Promised Land would be launched. There is an interval of thirty-seven years between Numbers 19:22 and 20:1.

THE FIRST MONTH: Although the year is not stated, at the end of Numbers 20 there is a report of the death of Aaron. According to Numbers 33:38, Aaron died on the first day of the fifth month of the fortieth year after the exodus from Egypt. Thus, the first month here must be the fortieth year. Most of the older generation had died in the wilderness by this point.

KADESH: Just as the people had begun their wilderness wanderings at Kadesh, so they ended them there. Kadesh was located on the northern boundary of the wilderness of Paran and on the southeast border of the wilderness of Zin.

MIRIAM DIED THERE: Moses' sister had led Israel in celebrating the victory over Egypt (see Exodus 15:20–21) but also led the attack against Moses recorded in Numbers 12:1–15. Her death served as a symbol that the old generation would not enter Canaan.

2. THERE WAS NO WATER: During Israel's forty years in the wilderness, water was their greatest physical need. The Lord had provided it continually, beginning at Horeb (see Exodus 17:1–7). Once again the people were faced with the identical test they had faced before, but instead of learning from that experience and trusting in God, they chose to again rebel against Moses and against the Lord.

3. WHEN OUR BRETHREN DIED: The people were referring to an incident that had occurred sometime before when a man named Korah led an uprising against Moses (see Numbers 16). The Lord had caused the earth to open and swallow Korah and his family, and more than 250 people were consumed in a divine fire. The next day, more people came to Moses and accused him of slaughtering Korah and his followers—so the Lord sent a devastating plague that wiped out more than 14,000 Israelites. The people were saying something truly dreadful by wishing they had been among those slain with Korah, for the Lord made it clear those people were accursed.

4. THAT WE AND OUR ANIMALS SHOULD DIE HERE: Once again, the people were falsely accusing God and Moses of planning to betray them—despite the fact that the Lord had miraculously sustained them for years in their wilderness wanderings.

5. TO BRING US TO THIS EVIL PLACE: The Israelites' complaints were quite astounding in their audacity. As slaves in Egypt, they had been treated with disdain and forced to make bricks without straw. The Lord was leading them to the Promised Land, a region flowing with milk and honey, and He had been abundantly faithful and gracious to them for years. Yet now they dared to suggest that the Promised Land was an evil place and that the Egypt of their slavery was better.

MOSES' ERROR: The Lord resolves the problem just as He had years before, except this time He instructs Moses not to strike the rock but to speak to it.

6. THEY FELL ON THEIR FACES: Moses' life was characterized by prayer. He was continually frustrated by the stubbornness and rebellion of the people, and he always responded by throwing himself before the Lord for guidance and strength. On this particular day, however, Moses would allow his temper to flare up.

8. SPEAK TO THE ROCK: The Lord had miraculously made water flow from a rock years before when the people were camped at Rephidim. At that time He directed Moses to *strike* the rock with his staff, but this time Moses was to *speak* to it.

10. YOU REBELS: Instead of speaking to the rock, Moses spoke to the people, accusing them of being rebels against God. Because of his actions, Moses joined the people in their rebellion (see Numbers 27:14).

MUST WE BRING WATER: Moses, in his exasperation and weariness, forgot that it was not his power that had worked so many miracles in the past. His life had always been distinguished by meekness, and he never took the glory to himself for the Lord's deeds, but on this occasion he lost sight of that fact. The consequences were severe.

11. MOSES LIFTED HIS HAND AND STRUCK THE ROCK: From a human perspective, this seems like a small error, but the Lord's word should never be treated lightly.

12. BECAUSE YOU DID NOT BELIEVE ME: The Lord's evaluation of Moses was that he had failed to take Him at His word and, thus, to treat Him as holy before the people. By disobeying the command of the Lord, Moses had demonstrated to the people that God was not worthy of obedience. Moses failed in the same way as Israel had failed at Kadesh thirty-eight years before.

YOU SHALL NOT BRING THIS ASSEMBLY INTO THE LAND: Moses' disobedience had been motivated by the same rebellious spirit that had motivated Korah and his followers. For this reason, God's judgment was that he would not take Israel into the land of Canaan. The inclusion of Aaron demonstrated his partnership with Moses in the action against the Lord.

Passage Denied: Moses is immediately hit with more bad news: the king of Edom flatly refuses to allow the Israelites to take an easier route through his land.

14. Moses sent messengers from Kadesh: The Israelites had camped at Kadesh to the west of Edomite territory (see the map in the Introduction). Moses wanted to take the easier passage across the Arabah to continue their journey around Moab and approach the land of Canaan from the east.

your brother Israel: The people of Edom were descended from Esau, the brother of Jacob (see Genesis 36:1). The Israelites recognized the Edomites as brethren and sent a cordial message to them.

17. the King's Highway: The major north-south trade route from the Gulf of Aqabah north to Damascus, which passed through the Edomite city of Sela. This road was constructed for caravans in addition to the king's armies.

20. with many men and with a strong hand: The king of Edom sent out his army to intercept Israel. Because the Israelites were forbidden by the Lord to engage in warfare with Edom (see Deuteronomy 2:4–6), they turned away from Edom's border.

Death of Aaron: Moses had lost his sister, and now he would lose his brother. Aaron's death further marks the passing of the first generation.

22. Mount Hor: This is most likely a mountain northeast of Kadesh on the border of Edom.

24. because you rebelled against My word: Again, God was referring to the fact that Aaron had joined Moses in rebellion when the congregation was camped in the wilderness of Zin. Aaron's death foreshadowed the death of Moses.

29. mourned for Aaron thirty days: Later, the Israelites would mourn for this same period of time when Moses died (see Deuteronomy 34:8). The normal time for mourning was seven days (see Genesis 50:10), so the extended length of this mourning revealed the importance of Aaron and the loss to Israel.

GOING DEEPER

Read Hebrews 11:23–29, noting the key words and phrases indicated below.

> HERO OF THE FAITH: *Even though Moses committed sin in disobeying God and striking the rock, he is still listed in the New Testament as a hero of the faith.*

23. BY FAITH MOSES: Moses was not perfect, and in this episode we certainly witness his human qualities. In spite of this, the author of Hebrew still considers him a model of faith to believers in Christ.

BEAUTIFUL CHILD: Meaning favored; in this case divinely favored (see Acts 7:20). The faith described here is actually that exercised by Moses' parents, although it is unclear how much Moses' parents understood about God's plan for their child.

24. REFUSED TO BE CALLED THE SON OF PHARAOH'S DAUGHTER: As we have seen, Moses was brought up by Pharaoh's daughter and treated like one of Pharaoh's family. He was in a position of high power and prestige and could easily have remained there the rest of his life. But he chose instead to identify with the Hebrews, the lowest class of slaves in Egypt. He never forgot that he was a Hebrew by birth and that the Lord had miraculously saved him from Pharaoh's decree of death to Hebrew males.

25. TO SUFFER AFFLICTION WITH THE PEOPLE OF GOD: Moses would have sinned had he refused to take on the responsibility God gave him regarding Israel, and he had a clear and certain conviction that "God would deliver them by his hand" (Acts 7:25). He endured the same hardships the Israelites experienced during their wilderness wanderings and suffered affliction from the people themselves. He endured their continual grumbling and rebellion while remaining faithful to God's commands.

ENJOY THE PASSING PLEASURES OF SIN: It is not sinful to enjoy legitimate pleasure in life, but it is sinful to lose sight of the fact that this world's enjoyments are temporary and will soon pass away. Moses gave up the many pleasures and privileges of his royal situation in Egypt because he knew the things of God are eternal. He had his eyes fixed on God's kingdom, not on man's kingdom.

26. **ESTEEMING THE REPROACH OF CHRIST:** Moses suffered reproach for the sake of Christ in the sense that he identified himself with the Lord's people in their suffering rather than with the household of Pharaoh. He also identified himself with Christ in his role as leader and prophet (see Deuteronomy 18:15). Anyone who suffers for his or her faith in God or for the gospel suffers for the sake of Christ. "If you are reproached for the name of Christ, blessed are you, for the Spirit of glory and of God rests upon you. On their part He is blasphemed, but on your part He is glorified" (1 Peter 4:14).

FOR HE LOOKED TO THE REWARD: Moses had his eyes fixed on the things of eternity, ignoring the present world and its allurements, "for he waited for the city which has foundations, whose builder and maker is God" (Hebrews 11:10).

27. **FORSOOK EGYPT:** Moses left Egypt the first time when he fled for his life after killing an Egyptian slave master (see Exodus 2:14–15). That time he *did* fear Pharaoh's wrath. On the second occasion, he turned his back on Egypt and all that it represented. This leaving was not for fear of Pharaoh, so this departure is the one in view here.

27. **HE ENDURED AS SEEING HIM WHO IS INVISIBLE:** Moses' faith was such that he responded to God's commands as though the Lord were standing visibly before him. This was the basis for his loyalty to God, and it should be a believer's example as well: "For our light affliction, which is but for a moment, is working for us a far more exceeding and eternal weight of glory, while we do not look at the things which are seen, but at the things which are not seen. For the things which are seen are temporary, but the things which are not seen are eternal" (2 Corinthians 4:17–18).

29. **RED SEA:** When the Israelites first reached the shores of the Red Sea, the people feared for their lives. But on hearing Moses' pronouncement of God's protection, they went forward in faith (see Exodus 14:11–14).

UNLEASHING THE TEXT

1) When have you faced hardship or deprivation? How did you respond?

_____

_____

_____

2) Why did the Israelites rebel against Moses the second time, even after seeing God provide water before? When have you done something similar?

_____

_____

_____

_____

3) If you had been in Moses' place, how would you have reacted to the Israelites in the second waterless episode?

_____

_____

_____

_____

4) Why did the Lord allow the people to get thirsty in the first place? What were His purposes in bringing water from the rock?

_____

_____

_____

_____

Exploring the Meaning

Jesus is the Rock of our salvation. The Lord provided water for His thirsting people by instructing Moses to strike a rock with his staff. This provided a picture of Christ, who was smitten by the rod of God's holy wrath—the Perfect

Man smitten for the sins of mankind. His blood flowed forth, providing the water of salvation to those who were dying of spiritual thirst.

As Jesus told the Samaritan woman in John 4:13, "Whoever drinks of this water [from the well] will thirst again, but whoever drinks of the water that I shall give him will never thirst. But the water that I shall give him will become in him a fountain of water springing up into everlasting life."

Those who embrace Jesus Christ as their Lord and Savior, wholly trusting in His sacrificial work on the cross, can be certain they have been forgiven from sin and given eternal life. "And this is eternal life, that they may know You, the only true God, and Jesus Christ whom You have sent" (John 17:3).

God's people must not take His commands lightly. Moses' life was characterized by faith and power, and he is listed in Hebrews 11 as one of the great people of God. But even he was not exempt from God's discipline. The Lord expected him to be an example to the people of what it meant to obey His word. When he disobeyed the Lord's command to speak to the rock, he disqualified himself from entering the Promised Land—a consequence that caused him deep grief.

From a human perspective, it seemed like a small failure when Moses struck the rock the second time. After all, he was under great duress from the Israelites' rebellion and complaints, and it is not surprising that he lost his temper once or twice. But the Lord expected Moses to be an example of obedience for the Israelites. God always holds those in leadership positions to a higher degree of accountability (see James 3:1). God expects His under-shepherds to be examples of faithfulness and obedience for others.

We do not know the larger implications of the Lord's work in our lives and circumstances. He may well be using our present situation to bring glory to Himself in ways that we never dreamed of. But whatever our situation, we must not take His commands lightly.

Our grumbling can have a negative effect on others. The people of Israel were constantly complaining during their exodus from Egypt. Even though the Lord had demonstrated His power and grace again and again, miraculously preserving them from their enemies and providing for their every need, they continuously accused Him of treachery.

It is a natural human response to complain when things go wrong in life. But whenever we do so, we are actually saying that we do not trust the Lord's sovereignty. We express a fear that He will prove unfaithful and that He is not worthy of our trust and obedience. Even small words of complaint can influence the people around us to stop trusting the Lord in their own lives.

For this reason, Paul instructed us to "do all things without complaining and disputing," that we may become "children of God without fault in the midst of a crooked and perverse generation, among whom [we] shine as lights in the world, holding fast the word of life" (Philippians 2:14–16).

REFLECTING ON THE TEXT

5) Why did God treat Moses' sin so severely? How did He show His grace?

_____

_____

_____

6) In what way did Moses fail to treat God as holy in front of the people? Why do you think Moses was held to such a strict accountability for his actions?

_____

_____

_____

7) In what ways is Christ pictured in the rock that provided water? How does the apostle Paul use this illustration in 1 Corinthians 10:1–4?

_____

_____

_____

8) God never abandoned the nation of Israel, even though they constantly complained against Him and Moses. What does this teach us about God's character? About His faithfulness?

_____

_____

_____

PERSONAL RESPONSE

9) How much does grumbling characterize your response to hardship? How might your words and attitude be influencing others?

_____

_____

_____

10) In what areas is the Lord calling you to trust Him more fully? In what areas is He calling you to greater obedience?

_____

_____

_____

11

BALAAM AND BALAK

Numbers 22:1–23:30; 25:1–3

DRAWING NEAR

Balaam was a false prophet who liked to dabble in the occult. How does our society often try to disguise the occult as something innocuous?

_____

_____

_____

THE CONTEXT

The Israelites had been wandering in the wilderness for many years, and they had finally camped near the Jordan River across from the city of Jericho. They had recently destroyed several Canaanite armies, and the Lord's power was abundantly evident to the world around them. The nations of Canaan were afraid of God's people!

One of those nations was Moab, whose people were descended from Lot. Years ago, the Lord had promised Lot that his descendants would enjoy an inheritance in the land of Canaan. He had, therefore, commanded the Israelites not to attack or disturb the Moabites or even to touch any of the land belonging to Moab. However, the leaders of Moab either didn't know about that injunction or placed no faith in it. They were afraid that Israel would destroy them, just as they had destroyed the surrounding nations.

So one Moabite leader, named Balak, decided that if he couldn't defeat the Israelites with physical force, he would fight them on the spiritual plane. He hired a world-renowned pagan prophet named Balaam to cast a curse on Israel. Balaam presents a picture of all those who dabble in the occult, and we discover that he was motivated not by a desire for truth but by a lust for monetary gain and worldly prestige.

The occult is real, but its powers are of the devil and will bring certain destruction on those who practice them. Fortunately, the power of God is far beyond the powers of the devil. What God blesses no power on earth or in hell can curse.

Keys to the Text

Read Numbers 22:1–23:30, noting the key words and phrases indicated below.

MEANWHILE, IN MOAB: The story of Israel's wanderings in the wilderness shifts focus to show us what is happening in nearby Moab.

1. THEN THE CHILDREN OF ISRAEL MOVED: This story took place well into the forty years of Israel's wandering in the wilderness, after both Aaron and Miriam had died.

THE PLAINS OF MOAB: Located near the Salt Sea (Dead Sea). See the map in the Introduction.

2. SAW ALL THAT ISRAEL HAD DONE TO THE AMORITES: The Israelites had utterly defeated the neighbors of Moab (see Numbers 21).

3. MOAB WAS SICK WITH DREAD: The sad irony of this verse was that the Lord had already forbidden the Israelites to attack the Moabites (see Deuteronomy 2:9). Balak actually had nothing to fear.

INTRODUCING BALAAM: Balaam is a pagan false prophet who earns a nice profit by interceding with false gods. He is in for some surprises this time.

5. BALAAM THE SON OF BEOR: Balaam was a false prophet who practiced divination and sorcery. He was from Pethor, a city on the Euphrates

River. It is likely this town was near Mari, where evidence has been found of a cult of prophets whose activities resembled those of Balaam. Balaam practiced magic and divination and eventually led Israel into apostasy. The New Testament writers would later identify Balaam as a false prophet (see 2 Peter 2:15–16; Jude 11).

6. CURSE THIS PEOPLE FOR ME: Balak immediately resorted to spiritism in hopes of defeating Israel. He had already recognized that the victories of Israel were due to the power of God, not to the strength of their army. Even so, Balak tried to fight the hand of God rather than submit to it.

HE WHOM YOU CURSE IS CURSED: A curse was an *imprecation*, or words that allegedly called down the anger of the gods on another person. Balaam apparently had a reputation for uttering curses that worked.

9. GOD CAME TO BALAAM: Balaam served the pagan gods of Canaan and made a tidy living charging for his services (see Numbers 22:7), which amounted to manipulating the supposed powers of his false gods to serve his needs. For this reason, it is astonishing that the Lord chose to appear to him at all. Balaam had no authority whatsoever to summon God this way. It is yet another demonstration of God's grace that He was even willing to speak to Balaam.

12. YOU SHALL NOT GO WITH THEM: The Lord mercifully gave Balaam instructions on what to do when He could have easily slain him on the spot. Balaam should have recognized that he was speaking to the one true God rather than the shams and false idols he had served in the past. He could have humbled himself before the Lord and found grace, but instead he continued to serve the god he had always served: money.

YOU SHALL NOT CURSE THE PEOPLE, FOR THEY ARE BLESSED: The Lord had promised Abraham, "I will bless those who bless you, and I will curse him who curses you; and in you all the families of the earth shall be blessed" (Genesis 12:3).

> UPPING THE ANTE: *Balak evidently knows Balaam's character and what motivates him. If Balaam will not come with the first offer, he will simply raise the price.*

13. THE LORD HAS REFUSED TO GIVE ME PERMISSION: If the story had ended here, Balaam (and Israel) would have been better off. But the devil has many wiles, and Balaam's temptation was not over.

15. MORE NUMEROUS AND MORE HONORABLE: Balak was determined to seduce Balaam to carry out his plan, so he resorted to flattery by sending emissaries who were more impressive—higher heads of state and glamorous celebrities, as it were. He evidently knew his man and understood what would get his attention. In fact, Balak may have assumed that Balaam's first refusal was merely a ploy to get more attention and a better fee. This suggests Balaam's selfish motives were well known.

18. I COULD NOT GO BEYOND THE WORD OF THE LORD MY GOD: This is far from the truth for two reasons: (1) the Lord was *not* the God whom Balaam served, and (2) Balaam would soon sell his services for much less than a "house full of silver and gold." His wheedling and bargaining with God demonstrate that he was not afraid to go against the Lord's directions. It is probable that Balaam was merely trying to impress his visitors by claiming to speak for yet another god.

19. WHAT MORE THE LORD WILL SAY: The Lord had already been emphatic in His instructions, so there was no need to ask a second time. But Balaam was sorely tempted by Balak's offer, and he was trying to wheedle God into letting him go.

20. RISE AND GO WITH THEM: Once again we see the grace of the Lord in His relations with humans—even with a man who did not truly acknowledge Him as God. The Lord relented to the point of allowing Balaam to go and earn his fee—but He warned him that he must take care to speak only what he was told.

BALAAM'S DONKEY: Balaam hardens his heart against God, just as Pharaoh had done in Egypt, and is motivated only by greed. His donkey will prove to be wiser than he.

22. GOD'S ANGER WAS AROUSED BECAUSE HE WENT: Balaam thought he could fool God in the same way he fooled men: by pretending to have one motivation while pursuing another. However, the Lord knew that Balaam intended to curse Israel for the highest fee, so He appeared to him unexpectedly to drive home His command. This time Balaam got the message.

AS AN ADVERSARY AGAINST HIM: God had previously appeared to Balaam in a somewhat compliant role, coming before him when summoned. Balaam did not realize this was due to the mercy of God, not to some power he wielded. In this confrontation, Balaam learned more about the character of the one true God.

23. THE DONKEY SAW THE ANGEL OF THE LORD: There is a delicious irony in the fact that Balaam, the world-renowned manipulator of the gods, could not even see what was evident to a donkey.

28. THE LORD OPENED THE MOUTH OF THE DONKEY: Even in His role as Balaam's adversary, the Lord still demonstrated His grace—even going to the point of working a wonderful miracle on Balaam's behalf.

29. YOU HAVE ABUSED ME: Literally, "you have made a fool of me." This was far truer than Balaam realized, for a donkey was about to instruct him in wisdom.

A SWORD IN MY HAND: Here is another humorous irony. Balaam did not realize there was indeed a sword nearby, but it was in the hand of an angel— and its potential victim was *not* the donkey!

31. FELL FLAT ON HIS FACE: Balaam was a diviner who played with forbidden powers he did not understand. For the first time in his life, he found himself face-to-face with the power of the one true God, and he was literally floored.

YOUR WAY IS PERVERSE: The Lord opens Balaam's eyes so he can finally see the truth. His desire for monetary gain is perverse in the Lord's eyes.

32. YOUR WAY IS PERVERSE BEFORE ME: The word translated *perverse* literally means "to push headlong or to drive recklessly." Balaam had heard the Lord's command not to curse Israel—indeed, not even to go with Balak's men—but he was stubbornly pushing forward. He was literally running ahead of the Lord, seeking his own way rather than waiting for the Lord's guidance or obeying it when he got it.

33. SURELY I WOULD ALSO HAVE KILLED YOU BY NOW: The Lord explicitly told Balaam that the only reason the false prophet was still breathing was because He had been extending His mercy.

34. IF IT DISPLEASES YOU: Even when face-to-face with the Angel of the Lord, Balaam persisted in being disingenuous. He already knew that it displeased God, yet he was stubbornly insisting on having his own way.

35. GO WITH THE MEN: God had already told Balaam what to do, but he had obstinately insisted on going with Balak's men. So the Lord permitted him

to continue on his way—but with the reiterated warning not to curse Israel. In the end, as we shall see, he found a way to disobey this command as well.

41. BROUGHT HIM UP TO THE HIGH PLACES OF BAAL: It is significant that Balaam looked on Israel from the worship sites dedicated to Canaan's false god. Balaam's entire outlook on life was from the perspective of Baal rather than the perspective of God. He remained spiritually blind for the rest of his life.

THE ORACLES OF BALAAM: *Balaam stands in the high place of Baal and pronounces not curses but blessings on Israel. The Lord uses the mouth of a pagan to speak truth.*

23:5. THE LORD PUT A WORD IN BALAAM'S MOUTH: Even though Balak and Balaam offered sacrifices on pagan altars, it was the Lord who gave Balaam his oracle.

7. HE TOOK UP HIS ORACLE: This statement introduces each of Balaam's speeches.

8. HOW SHALL I CURSE WHOM GOD HAS NOT CURSED: This is a tremendous truth for God's people: those whom God has blessed cannot be cursed. Neither the world, other people, nor the devil himself can bring lasting harm to those under God's blessings.

9. FROM THE TOP OF THE ROCKS I SEE HIM: Even from elevated heights of wicked power where Balaam was standing, he could do nothing to harm God's people.

NOT RECKONING ITSELF AMONG THE NATIONS: God's people are separate from the world around them. They are not part of the world's system.

10. WHO CAN COUNT THE DUST OF JACOB: The Lord had promised Abraham, "I will make your descendants as the dust of the earth; so that if a man could number the dust of the earth, then your descendants also could be numbered" (Genesis 13:16).

LET ME DIE THE DEATH OF THE RIGHTEOUS: This may have been a sincere wish of Balaam, but it did not come to pass. He may have desired the reward of the righteous, but he lived the life of the self-serving. His end was the death of the wicked.

19. GOD IS NOT A MAN, THAT HE SHOULD LIE: Balaam's second oracle is a wonderful revelation of God's character. He never lies, and His promises never fail.

23. THERE IS NO SORCERY AGAINST JACOB: Balaam and Balak believed that they could use sorcery and other forbidden magical practices to bring a curse against God's people, but they were only using the devil's tools—and those tools are utterly powerless against God's people.

OH, WHAT GOD HAS DONE: The majesty of God's sovereign work leaves one speechless. God's ways are glorious and beyond the comprehension of man.

28. PEOR: Also named Beth Peor (see Deuteronomy 3:29), it was the location of a temple to Baal.

Read Numbers 25:1–3, noting the key words and phrases indicated below.

BALAAM EARNS HIS PROFIT: Balaam is not permitted to openly curse Israel, but he finds another way to earn his money: by advising Balak to seduce Israel to sin.

25:1. NOW ISRAEL REMAINED IN ACACIA GROVE: The focus now shifts from Balaam, standing atop the high places of Baal, to the people of Israel in the plain below. Acacia Grove, where the Israelites were situated, was a region across the Jordan River from Jericho, from where Israel would later invade the land of Canaan (see Joshua 2:1). The events that follow would have taken place not long after Balaam uttered his oracles.

THE PEOPLE BEGAN TO COMMIT HARLOTRY WITH THE WOMEN OF MOAB: The people of Moab undertook this plan based on advice from Balaam (see Numbers 31:16). In the end, Balaam was not able to openly speak a curse against Israel, but he earned his filthy profit by counseling the Moabites to undermine Israel's sexual morals. The devil still works this way, seducing God's people into embracing the ways of the world.

2. THEY INVITED THE PEOPLE TO THE SACRIFICES: These sacrifices included fertility rites involving sexual immorality. Although God's people are not to be unfriendly to non-Christians, neither are we to adopt their ways and perspectives (see James 4:4).

UNLEASHING THE TEXT

1) Why did Balak hire Balaam to curse Israel? In what ways was this a foolish deed?

_____

_____

_____

2) What motivated Balaam?

_____

_____

_____

3) Why was Balaam unable to curse Israel?

_____

_____

_____

4) How did Balaam finally earn his money?

_____

_____

_____

EXPLORING THE MEANING

No power on earth or in hell can stand against God's blessing. Balaam wanted to cast a curse on God's people. It was how he earned his living, and he stood to make a handsome profit from the people of Moab. He even represented supposedly powerful false gods such as Baal and had every advantage the world could bring to bear against Israel. Yet he was unable to pronounce anything other than a blessing.

God has placed His blessing on those who are redeemed by the blood of Christ. When He looks on us, He views us through that filter—He sees only the holiness of Jesus, not our sins and shortcomings. There is nothing on earth or in hell or even in heaven itself that can ever undo God's blessing on His people. What Christ accomplished on the cross can never be undone.

As Paul wrote, "I am persuaded that neither death nor life, nor angels nor principalities nor powers, nor things present nor things to come, nor height nor depth, nor any other created thing, shall be able to separate us from the love of God which is in Christ Jesus our Lord" (Romans 8:38–39).

God's people must stand guard against the temptations of the world. The opposite side to the first principle is that even Christians are in constant danger of falling into the world's sinful pattern. The devil lays many traps to ensnare God's people. He cannot have our souls, but he can lead us into error if we do not stand guard.

Balaam recognized this truth, and he taught the Moabites how to seduce God's people through pagan practices. The Israelites fell into the temptation of sexual immorality due in large part to Balaam's advice. Balaam himself was led to destruction through his own love of money and perhaps his fear of men. But Jesus said, "My friends, do not be afraid of those who kill the body, and after that have no more that they can do. But I will show you whom you should fear: Fear Him who, after He has killed, has power to cast into hell; yes, I say to you, fear Him!" (Luke 12:4–5).

Peter also had a dire warning for those who would follow God: "Be sober, be vigilant; because your adversary the devil walks about like a roaring lion, seeking whom he may devour. Resist him, steadfast in the faith, knowing that the same sufferings are experienced by your brotherhood in the world" (1 Peter 5:8–9).

Do not dabble in the occult. Balaam was just one of many false prophets in Canaan during his day. These people used various forms of magic and sorcery to speak with false gods (demons) and to "tap into" the power of the spirit realm. What they didn't realize, however, was that they were not interacting with any gods at all but with the power of Satan.

Interest in the occult is on the rise in Western society today, and even Christians are being lured into dabbling with spirit guides, channeling, horoscopes, praying to angels, and other elements of magic. These are not innocent toys to play with, nor are they legitimate powers that mankind has at his disposal. They are forms of sorcery, and the power behind them is the devil.

God forbids His people from any contact with such things. "There shall not be found among you anyone who . . . practices witchcraft, or a soothsayer, or one who interprets omens, or a sorcerer, or one who conjures spells, or a medium, or a spiritist, or one who calls up the dead. For all who do these things are an abomination to the LORD" (Deuteronomy 18:10–12).

REFLECTING ON THE TEXT

5) What does God reveal about His character through the story of Balaam? What do we learn of human nature?

_____

_____

_____

6) Why did God use a pagan false prophet to speak truth? What does this reveal about His sovereignty?

_____

_____

_____

7) How might the Israelites have avoided sin with the Moabites? What could they have done to stand firm against that temptation?

_____

_____

_____

8) What temptations does the world offer that draw us away from God? What can we do to protect ourselves? (See Ephesians 6:10–18 for a helpful starting point.)

_____

_____

_____

PERSONAL RESPONSE

9) What are some areas of the occult that are popular in the world today? How should Christians respond to such things?

_____

_____

_____

10) Read Romans 8:38–39. Which of the things on this list are most meaningful to you? Spend time today praising God for His great love.

_____

_____

_____

12

Reviewing Key Principles

Drawing Near

As you look back at each of the studies in Exodus and Numbers, what is
the one thing that stood out to you most? What is one new perspective you
have learned?

_____

_____

_____

The Context

In the preceding eleven studies, we have covered an important period of Israel's
history. There is much more in the Pentateuch about Israel's wanderings in the
wilderness, yet in these few glimpses we have seen again and again that the
Lord is faithful to His promises and always provides for His people.

We have also seen the sad truth that God's people are quick to become dis-
contented and quick to rebel against the Lord's leadership. In fact, Israel's rebellion against God was a recurring theme practically from their first day as freed
slaves. Yet from their story, we can glean some valuable principles that, if heeded,
will mean the difference between God's frown and God's favor on our lives.

Here are a few of the major themes we have found. Again, there are many more we don't have room to reiterate, so take some time to review the earlier studies—or, better still, to meditate on the passages in Scripture that we have covered. As you do, remember to ask the Holy Spirit to give you wisdom and insight into His Word.

EXPLORING THE MEANING

We must not harden our hearts against God's Word. Pharaoh repeatedly refused to obey God's commands to let the Israelites leave Egypt, yet the Lord continued to give him opportunities to repent. Eventually, however, the Lord gave Pharaoh over to his hardness of heart and allowed him to remain in stubborn rebellion.

The same principle is true today for the lost world around us. We are living in the day of grace, when salvation is freely available to all who believe, but that day will not last forever. The day is coming when the time for repentance will end. In that dark day, all who have rejected Christ will be cast out of the presence of God for all eternity.

It is a dangerous matter to resist God's grace. Each time a person refuses to repent, that act of repentance becomes more difficult. Those who need to repent must do it *now*: "For He says: 'In an acceptable time I have heard you, and in the day of salvation I have helped you.' Behold, now is the accepted time; behold, now is the day of salvation" (2 Corinthians 6:2).

Never forget what the Lord has done. The people of Israel had seen the Lord perform many amazing miracles as He demonstrated His power and determination to set them free from slavery. He had sent ten plagues that devastated Egypt while leaving the Israelites unharmed. He had spoken to them through Moses, predicting that Pharaoh would drive them out of Egypt, heavily laden with gold and silver—and it had happened exactly as promised. Yet when the first setback occurred, they instantly forgot all those signs and wonders and accused God of betraying them.

This is a characteristic that is common to fallen human nature. We rejoice when the Lord blesses us and give Him glory for His loving intervention in our lives. But then something goes wrong, or some unexpected threat arises, and we are immediately filled with fear and doubt. We wonder if the Lord has abandoned us, or we simply forget to trust Him and try instead to solve the matter by our own power.

It is vital for us to remember what the Lord has done in our lives so we don't become fearful when circumstances go against us. If the Lord was faithful in the past, we can be confident that He will be faithful in the future. "Beware that you do not forget the LORD your God by not keeping His commandments, His judgments, and His statutes which I command you today" (Deuteronomy 8:11). "Bless the LORD, O my soul, and forget not all His benefits" (Psalm 103:2).

We are to fear God, not man. Pharaoh was the most powerful man in the most powerful nation on earth. His army was feared around the known world, and they were equipped with the latest technologies and the best-trained armies. The Israelites, on the other hand, were newly released slaves with no military experience and no chariots. It is no wonder they were frightened when they looked behind them and saw the great dust cloud of Pharaoh's army bearing down on them.

But the greatest army on earth is no match for the power of God. The Lord led Pharaoh's army into the Red Sea and then plucked the wheels off their chariots as simply as a man snaps a toothpick. At the same time, He led His people *through* the sea on dry ground. They did not even get their feet wet!

Our tendency is to focus on what we can see and to believe the evidence of our senses. But the Lord calls us to walk by faith and to rely fully on His unlimited power and His faithfulness. "In God I have put my trust; I will not be afraid. What can man do to me?" (Psalm 56:11). "For He Himself has said, 'I will never leave you nor forsake you.' So we may boldly say: 'The Lord is my helper; I will not fear. What can man do to me?'" (Hebrews 13:5–6).

The Ten Commandments are summarized by the two greatest commandments. The Lord summarized His moral law for the people of Israel by giving them the Ten Commandments. In the New Testament, Jesus summarized them even further when a young man asked Him, "Teacher, which is the great commandment in the law?"

Jesus' reply to the man was, "'You shall love the Lord your God with all your heart, with all your soul, and with all your mind.' This is the first and great commandment. And the second is like it: 'You shall love your neighbor as yourself.' On these two commandments hang all the Law and the Prophets" (Matthew 22:36–40).

The Ten Commandments fall into these two categories. Some of them spell out what it means to love God with all our hearts, souls, and minds, while others give practical ways of loving our neighbors as we do ourselves. These two principles summarize what it means to live a godly life. Keeping the Law will not bring us redemption for sin—only the death of Christ, God's Passover Lamb, can accomplish that—but Christians *are* called to put these two principles into action in all areas of life.

"For the commandments, 'You shall not commit adultery,' 'You shall not murder,' 'You shall not steal,' 'You shall not bear false witness,' 'You shall not covet,' and if there is any other commandment, are all summed up in this saying, namely, 'You shall love your neighbor as yourself.' Love does no harm to a neighbor; therefore love is the fulfillment of the law" (Romans 13:9–10).

Contentment is a choice. The Lord led His people into the wilderness, a desert region devoid of food and water, and wanted them to live there for a short time in order to show how He would provide for all their needs. He rained manna down on them twice a day and provided water miraculously. But the people grew tired of manna and started to complain about eating "nothing at all except this manna before our eyes" (Numbers 11:6). They also began to complain about not having any meat.

This demonstrates an important principle of happiness: we *choose* whether or not we will be content. Contentment comes when we remember to be grateful for what the Lord has given us. If the Israelites had remembered each day to praise the Lord for His miraculous provision of food and water—focusing on the good things they *did* have—they would not have focused on the meat they *didn't* have. They would have been content, and the Lord would have been glorified.

Paul wrote, "I have learned in whatever state I am, to be content" (Philippians 4:11). This is a good pattern for God's people to emulate. "Godliness with contentment is great gain. For we brought nothing into this world, and it is certain we can carry nothing out. And having food and clothing, with these we shall be content. But those who desire to be rich fall into temptation and a snare, and into many foolish and harmful lusts which drown men in destruction and perdition" (1 Timothy 6:6–9).

Rebellion is like the sin of witchcraft. The Lord's response to rebellion among the Israelites was swift and strong. Miriam was stricken instantly with leprosy (see Numbers 12), Korah and his followers were swallowed up by the earth (see Numbers 16), and fire rained from heaven and burned a portion of the Israelite camp (see Numbers 11). The Lord hates a rebellious spirit, just as He hates witchcraft.

The reason for this is that a rebellious spirit is actually the same in its essence as witchcraft and idolatry. When we grumble and complain about the Lord's provision in our lives, we are rebelling against His leadership and authority. When we rebel against the Lord, we are setting ourselves up in His place as lord of our lives. This is the same sin that Satan committed when he declared himself to be equal with God.

God has pronounced woe on all who rebel against Him—even His own people: "'Woe to the rebellious children,' says the LORD, 'who take counsel, but not of Me, and who devise plans, but not of My Spirit, that they may add sin to sin'" (Isaiah 30:1). Worse, he considers every rebel his *foe* and actually fights them: "But they rebelled and grieved His Holy Spirit; so He turned Himself against them as an enemy, and He fought against them" (Isaiah 63:10).

God's people are to be of good courage. God's Word frequently commands us to be of good courage and not succumb to fear. These are *commands*, not suggestions or mere words of encouragement. At times the emotion of fear can come on us whether we will it or not. However, what we do with that fear *is* a matter of our will and a matter of obedience to God's command.

Joshua and Caleb saw the same giants that the other ten spies saw. They examined the same walled cities and observed the same trained enemy armies—and yet they came to a radically different conclusion. The reason was that Joshua and Caleb deliberately resisted and overcame their fear, while the other ten fell prey to it.

We resist fear by consciously focusing our minds on the promises and character of God, not on the seemingly insurmountable problems that we face. We also resist fear by remembering the many ways in which God has been faithful to us in the past and by choosing to trust Him to continue to be faithful in the future. In a phrase, we resist fear simply by *choosing* to trust God.

Do not dabble in the occult. Balaam was just one of many false prophets in Canaan during his day. These people used various forms of magic and sorcery to speak with false gods (demons) and to "tap into" the power of the spirit realm. What they didn't know, however, was that they were not interacting with any gods at all, but rather with the power of Satan.

Interest in the occult is on the rise in Western society today, and even Christians are being lured into dabbling with spirit guides, channeling, horoscopes, praying to angels, and other elements of magic. These things are not innocent toys to play with, nor are they legitimate powers that mankind has at his disposal. They are forms of sorcery, and the power behind them is the devil.

God forbids His people from any contact with such things. "There shall not be found among you anyone who . . . practices witchcraft, or a soothsayer, or one who interprets omens, or a sorcerer, or one who conjures spells, or a medium, or a spiritist, or one who calls up the dead. For all who do these things are an abomination to the LORD" (Deuteronomy 18:10–12).

UNLEASHING THE TEXT

1) Which of the concepts or principles in this study have you found to be the most encouraging? Why?

_____

_____

_____

2) Which of the concepts or principles have you found most challenging? Why?

_____

_____

_____

3) What aspects of "walking with God" are you already doing in your life? Which areas need strengthening?

_____

_____

_____

4) To which of the characters that we've studied have you most been able to relate? How might you emulate that person in your own life?

_____

_____

_____

PERSONAL RESPONSE

5) Have you taken a definite stand for Jesus Christ? Have you accepted His free gift of salvation? If not, what is preventing you from doing so?

_____

_____

_____

6) In what areas of your life have you been most convicted during this study? What exact things will you do to address these convictions? Be specific.

_____

_____

_____

7) What have you learned about the character of God during this study? How has this insight affected your worship or prayer life?

_____

_____

_____

8) What are some specific things that you want to see God do in your life in the coming month? What are some things that you intend to change in your own life during that time? (Return to this list in one month and hold yourself accountable to fulfill these things.)

_____

_____

_____

If you would like to continue in your study of the Old Testament, read the next title in this series: *Joshua, Judges, and Ruth: Finally in the Land.*

ALSO AVAILABLE

I n this study, John MacArthur guides readers through an in-depth look at the creation story, the first murder, Noah and the Flood, the first covenant, the Tower of Babel, and the dispersion of the nations. This study includes close-up examinations of Adam, Eve, Cain, Abel, and Noah, as well as careful considerations of doctrinal themes such as "The Fall of Man" and "Heritage and Family."

The MacArthur Bible Studies provide intriguing examinations of the whole of Scripture. Each guide incorporates extensive commentary, detailed observations on overriding themes, and probing questions to help you study the Word of God with guidance from John MacArthur.

ALSO AVAILABLE

I n this study, John MacArthur guides readers through an in-depth look at the historical period beginning with Abraham's call from God, continuing through his relocation in the land of Canaan, and concluding with the story of his grandsons Jacob and Esau. This study includes close-up examinations of Sarah, Hagar, Ishmael, and Isaac, as well as careful considerations of doctrinal themes such as "Covenant and Obedience" and "Wrestling with God."

The MacArthur Bible Studies provide intriguing examinations of the whole of Scripture. Each guide incorporates extensive commentary, detailed observations on overriding themes, and probing questions to help you study the Word of God with guidance from John MacArthur.

ALSO AVAILABLE

JOHN MACARTHUR

GENESIS
34–50

JACOB AND EGYPT

MacArthur Bible Studies

I n this study, John MacArthur guides readers through an
in-depth look at the historical period beginning with
Jacob's first encounter with Rachel, continuing through their
son Joseph's captivity as an Egyptian slave, and concluding
with the dramatic rescue of Jacob's family. This study
includes close-up examinations of Dinah (Jacob's daughter),
Judah, Tamar, and Pharaoh's chief butler, as well as careful
considerations of doctrinal themes such as "The Sovereignty
of God" and "Finishing in Faith."

The MacArthur Bible Studies provide intriguing examinations of the whole of Scripture. Each guide incorporates
extensive commentary, detailed observations on overriding
themes, and probing questions to help you study the Word of
God with guidance from John MacArthur.